A Good Death

A Good Death

TAKING MORE CONTROL AT
THE END OF YOUR LIFE

Choice In Dying
the national council
for the right to die

◆

T. Patrick Hill

David Shirley

A MERLOYD LAWRENCE BOOK

▲▼ Addison-Wesley Publishing Company, Inc.

Reading, Massachusetts • Menlo Park, California • New York
Don Mills, Ontario • Wokingham, England • Amsterdam • Bonn
Sydney • Singapore • Tokyo • Madrid • San Juan
Paris • Seoul • Milan • Mexico City • Taipei

Library of Congress Cataloging-in-Publication Data

Hill, T. Patrick.
    A good death : taking more control at the end of your life /
  Choice In Dying, Inc.—the national council for the right to die : T.
  Patrick Hill, David Shirley.
      p. cm.
    "A Merloyd Lawrence book."
    Includes bibliographical references (p.) and index.
    ISBN 0-201-06223-2 (pbk.)
    1. Terminal care. 2. Death—Psychological aspects. I. Shirley,
  David A. II. Choice In Dying, Inc. (Organization : U.S.) III. Title.
  R726.8.H55 1992
  362.1'75—dc20   92-3803
                                                  CIP

Cover design by Stephen Gleason
Text design by Diane Levy
Copy edited by Sharon Sharp
Set in 11-point Galliard by Ampersand

1 2 3 4 5 6 7 8 9-MA-95949392
First printing, July 1992

Contents

Acknowledgments

One could be forgiven for thinking that a book is written by its author. In many cases that may be true. But in the case of *A Good Death*, it would be truer to say that without the indispensable assistance of Diana Bader, June Bingham, James Booher, Denis Brodeur, Molly Cooke, Laird Covey, Jeanne Dennis, Elliot Dorff, Rita Dyer, David Finley, Joseph Kukura, John Daido Loori, Diane Meier, Mary Meyer, William Nelson, Kathleen Nolan, David Smith, Russell Portenoy, Lucy Piñero, and Kenneth Zysk, the book as conceived would not have seen the light of day. We are indebted to them, a debt of which we can be proud.

We are also grateful to Fenella Rouse, first for her vote of confidence in asking us to write the book; second, for all the support necessary for the successful completion of the work.

Without the unfailing courtesy, patience, and wisdom of Merloyd Lawrence, that work would not have been half the fun it was. And the work would never have got under way if it had not been for the vision of A. J. Levinson and the late Gertrude Macy who first interested the publishers in the idea of the book and then persuaded them of its real need.

My greatest debt is to my wife AnnMarie and our children Katya and St. John. They in a thousand unsuspected, eloquent ways give voice to what lies at the heart of this book—a whole life.

—T. Patrick Hill

I would like to express my gratitude to Clarence Collins, for his patience, his tireless sense of irony, and his not-so-subtle mentoring, even in the face of his own dying; and to Patty Naegely, whose perfect mix of kindness and skepticism kept me close to the things that matter. I would also like to thank and acknowledge all the members of the Collab, both teachers and students, especially Carol, Mick, Bob, Jeanne, and J.B.

—David Shirley

Preface

Eight years ago, when I first started working in what is called the "right to die" field, I was impressed with the vehemence people displayed when talking about the kind of dying they wanted to have. There was very little uncertainty in the minds of the people I met—they were sure that they did not want to linger in an unconscious or semi-conscious state, and personal dignity was often high on the list of things they wanted to keep. To be honest, I found it hard to understand why this was so important to so many people. Wouldn't being alive and feeling sunlight more than outweigh the physical indignity of wearing diapers or being restrained in a bed or chair?

Now I see it differently, as I have come to realize that living our lives is a creative act for most of us. We are a central character in a story we write ourselves, and it is not so much what happens to us but how we feel about it that gives our life shape and meaning. If we rob people of choice at the end of their lives we take away their individuality. If we force people to live in a way that is antithetical to all they have cared about, to all their ideas of their own identity, we do indeed offer a fate worse than death. To ignore personal choice is an act of real violence because it tramples personality. And for many of us the possibility of existing in a state in which we can no longer take part in crafting our own lives is a horrifying prospect that invalidates all the hard work we put into being conscious human beings.

Trainee volunteers in hospice programs are often asked to take part in an exercise that mirrors what many people feel at the end of their lives. The things one values most in life are written, one by one, on ten separate pieces of paper. They might be the names of people, or sensations—for instance the feel of sunlight—or perceptions like listening to music or seeing color. They might involve physical activity, traveling, hiking, or painting. They might be characteristics of one's life such as independence, or the feeling of being part of a family, the ability to make one's own decisions, or the support of a spouse, friend, or child. The ten pieces of paper are held in one's hand, cradled and appreciated for a moment or two and then, one by one, thrown away. It is an agonizingly difficult experience, choosing which to jettison first and feeling the loss as it goes. Of course, in real life, we don't get to choose which treasures to keep for a little bit longer and which we let go. I was in tears the first time I did this, which is not uncommon, and filled with rage at the person or fate that was making me do it. But the exercise is also a revelation. Until I did it I had not fully realized how impoverished a life without music would be for me. I would manage, of course, as one does, but I now know that if I have any choice I would like to hold on to listening to music as long as I can.

Contemplation of death in 1992 has a different flavor from the same activity in the past. Now we are concerned not only with the acceptance of our own mortality, and what that means for each of us, but we also plan actively for the practical details of the period that precedes our death in a way that I think has never occurred before. As we all know, many of us will live for much longer than our forbears and our family structures have changed. Financial planning for the last phase of our lives has become commonplace for many and we also give thought to the kind of housing that might be most suitable in our seventies, eighties, and nineties. Health care costs are an issue for all of us, regardless of the age at which we die. Medicine offers us more than ever before. As a result of these changes, contemplation of death now has a practical component as well as its traditional spiritual and existential aspects.

A wise friend of mine reminds me that humor is one of the indicators of being a human being and that nurturing it as long as we can is a way of acknowledging the human spirit. Just as I hope that we can draw back from the transformation of death into a medical event, rather than a human experience, so I hope that the current interest in planning for dying doesn't take on a pessimistic tone. In a perfect world we will have realistic information about our options, give them serious consideration, make the choices that suit us best, and then live hard, smiling when we can, for every moment that remains.

Fenella Rouse, J.D.
Executive Director,
Choice In Dying: the
national council for
the right to die

ONE

Prologue

A good death does honor to a whole life.
PETRARCH

In a comfortable middle-class suburb in California, a family of five is suddenly torn apart when the youngest child, a twenty-year-old college freshman, is critically injured in an automobile accident. Massive injuries, including a crushed skull and prolonged blood loss, leave the young man disfigured, permanently unconscious, and dependent for his continued survival on both a respirator and a feeding tube. Two older sisters, convinced that their brother would not wish to live under such conditions, insist that the respirator be removed. The parents, however, are equally adamant that all treatment be continued. "As long as there's life, there's hope," recites the mother emphatically, over the repeated objections of her daughters. After several months the boy is finally moved to a nursing home, where his condition remains unchanged.

On the streets of a large northeastern city, Mrs. G., an eighty-three-year-old Latino woman collapses from a cardiac arrest. She is taken by ambulance to the emergency room of a nearby medical center. En route, cardiopulmonary resuscitation (CPR) is aggressively applied by the paramedics just in time to restore her life, but not her consciousness. Later in the day, Mrs. G. is transferred to the hospital's intensive care unit, where she is put on mechanical ventilation to allow her to continue breathing. Her only remaining relative, a distressed but articulate niece, arrives that night.

1

The niece informs a sympathetic house staff and the attending physician that her aunt, whom she has never seen ill, had on several occasions made her promise that she would not let her be kept alive "once her time had come." Satisfied with the young woman's sincerity and the unquestionably grim prognosis, the attending physician formally recommends that all life-sustaining treatment be removed. The hospital administration, however, repeatedly denies the request.

In a private hospital in the Midwest, a teenage girl is slowly and painfully dying of bone cancer. Both the girl and the rest of her family are devoutly Orthodox Jewish. The doctors and nurses are convinced that the father speaks for the entire family when he repeatedly demands to those providing her care, "Only when we have done everything that is humanly possible to save her—only then will we know that her death is God's will." Yet, without exception, the medical staff regard any further aggressive treatment as both useless and inhumane. All of the staff—especially the young attending physician—feel torn between their respect for this family's beliefs and their awareness of the needless suffering that continued treatment will cause the girl.

For most of us, the stories are all too familiar. We've all read them on the front page of the newspaper, heard them on the nightly news, even seen them dramatized in the latest made-for-television movie. For many of us, the issues are even more real and the problems described much closer to home. Far too many of us have watched in anguished disbelief as someone we love has faced death in a sterile institutional setting, cut off from the people and things that might have given security and comfort, and hooked up to machines and other technical equipment that seemed to do little more than prolong the process of dying.

Such experiences have moved large numbers of us to say, "Enough is enough." The way that terminally ill patients are commonly treated in our health-care system is being questioned across the country. Increasingly, people both in and out of the medical profession have begun to examine many of the assumptions and basic convictions that have guided medical practice for most of the last half of this century: that brute physical life should be preserved at all costs, regardless of the suffering or impairment that may accompany it; that doctors always know what is best for their patients; that death is a form of failure.

With such questioning, of course, comes responsibility. Challenging and changing the old system of care requires that we not only become familiar with our own medical histories but also learn about the possible treatments that we can most likely anticipate with serious illness or advanced age. It requires that we examine—in the company of family, friends, and others whose feelings and opinions we value—our own convictions and beliefs *before* the onset of a crisis. Further, it requires that we learn—in advance of the need—as much as possible about the law, the policies of institutions, and the attitudes and practices of those who will most likely treat us.

In order to challenge and change current practices, we must first accept a hard lesson that many of us spend our lives trying to avoid: that death is and will continue to be a part of life, regardless of future discoveries in medical technology, of the outcomes of new legislation or court rulings, of the impact of current movements for patient empowerment, or of the latest how-to manual on planning for the end of life. The sudden trauma of a critical injury, the suffering and loss of control brought on by chronic terminal illness, the pain and indignities of aging—we all will face one or more of these. As important as the legal, medical, and educational efforts are and will continue to be, they are no substitute for the difficult work of reflection and self-education that we all must do. Nor will they reduce the crucial importance of communicating and documenting our wishes for our end-of-life care, both for those we love and for those who will be responsible for that care.

Not all of the readers of this book will have the luxury of reading, reflecting, and preparing before terminal illness strikes in the family. If such is the case, readers may choose to skip to chapters 3, 4, 5, and 6 and consult with Choice In Dying (see appendix) about the documents necessary in their state before reading and reflecting upon the whole book.

TWO

The End of Life
and the Law

Teach us to number our days.
PSALM 90:12

In January 1983, twenty-four-year-old Nancy Cruzan suffered permanent brain damage in an automobile accident near her home in Jasper County, Missouri. Diagnosed as being in a "persistent and irreversible vegetative state," Cruzan was committed to the care of a Missouri state hospital, where it was estimated that she could continue living for another thirty years with the assistance of artificial hydration (provision of the fluids necessary for life) and nutrition. After she had lived for several years in this condition, Lester and Joyce Cruzan, her parents, petitioned for a court order to have Nancy removed from the equipment that was keeping her alive. The Missouri Court ruled that the parents' insistence that their daughter would not want to continue living under such conditions failed to meet the standard of "clear and convincing evidence" that it required in cases involving the withdrawal of treatment from once competent patients. (Nancy Cruzan had not written a living will or other advance directive.) The U.S. Supreme Court later upheld this high evidentiary standard, finding that there was a constitutionally protected right to refuse treatment but that the state could ask for a high evidentiary standard to confirm that the decision being implemented is, in fact, what the patient would want.

For many, the U.S. Supreme Court's decision represented a setback for patients' rights advocates and proponents of the right to die. At the same time, however, the opinions of the concurring and dissenting justices, constituting a clear majority of the Court, recognized that a competent adult patient has a constitutional right to reject unwanted medical treatment. In order to understand the importance of the Court's decision for advance directives and other forms of end-of-life decision making, we need to explore further the legal and conceptual background of the patient self-determination movement.

"The right to be free from medical attention without consent," wrote U.S. Supreme Court Justice William Brennan in his dissenting opinion to the Court's 1990 ruling on *Missouri v. Cruzan,* "to determine what shall be done with one's own body, is deeply rooted in this nation's tradition."[1] In fact, as the majority opinion in that historic case conceded, a competent patient's right to refuse unwanted medical treatment is derived from our common-law traditions of bodily integrity and informed consent, in which "even the touching of one person by another without consent and without legal justification was a battery."[2]

In 1914, New York Court of Appeals Justice Benjamin Cardozo, in the case of *Schloendorff v. Society of New York Hospital,* articulated one of the earliest applications of these twin traditions to the legal rights of a patient considering treatment. "Every human being of adult years and sound mind," wrote Justice Cardozo, "has a right to determine what shall be done with his own body; and a surgeon who performs an operation without his patient's consent commits an assault, for which he is liable in damages."[3] In a very narrow and literal sense, the rights of patients to manage their own health care were assured once and for all with that decision, at least in principle. Certainly Justice Cardozo's ruling cemented the principle that the "bodily interest" of the competent adult individual is not limited by social, medical, or legal criteria. The decision to receive or forego medical treatment is a personal, and not a medical, one. Each one of us may decide what type of care to seek or to refuse.

The problems, of course, have not been with the law itself (or with the principles of bodily integrity and informed consent that inform the law) but with the way it is carried out in the actual, daily care of terminally ill patients. For twenty years, U.S. courts and state legislatures have worked to sharpen and define the legal meaning of and the limits to such important concepts as "competency," "informed consent," and "substituted judgment." In order to prepare a living will and put it to work, one must understand these terms.

INFORMED CONSENT

Simply put, the doctrine of informed consent requires that patients, in order to make reasonable treatment decisions that are in their own best interests, must be given the following information: (1) a thorough description of the patient's present condition and the potential risks of nontreatment; (2) a description of the procedures involved in, as well as the potential risks and benefits of, the recommended treatment; and (3) any available alternatives to the recommended treatment.[4] On paper, at least, the doctrine seems perfectly reasonable (one cannot make an "informed" decision without access to information), and easy enough for physicians to implement.

For decades, however, physicians rarely informed their patients of a terminal diagnosis, depriving them of the possibility of having any say in how their treatment would be handled. The main reason for this was that in most cases there were few, if any, curative therapies available for life-threatening illnesses. The physician's role (often assisted by family members and friends) was simply to make the terminally ill person as comfortable as possible as death approached, protecting the patient from any unnecessary suffering or distress. Most people—physicians and the general public alike—felt that protecting the patient meant withholding from patients the painful news of their terminal condition. Over time, certain myths arose around this practice, chief among them the generally untested conviction that a patient would lose all hope and die in needless pain and despair if informed of a terminal diagnosis. The main thing to remember here is that the intent of the physician in withholding details about a patient's condition, rooted in an undeniable paternalism, was to protect the patient (and arguably the physician) from discomfort. Physicians were not trying to subject patients to potentially unwanted treatments without their consent.

With the remarkable developments in pharmacology and medical technology (such as mechanical ventilation and cardiopulmonary resuscitation, or CPR) during the 1940s and 1950s, all this changed. Almost overnight, the role of the physician was transformed from one who eased symptoms and comforted the patient in the face of death to one who healed all illnesses and conquered death. Armed with new technology and treatment procedures, many physicians, who had previously been forced to stand by helplessly as their seriously ill patients died, began to see disease and death as obstacles to be challenged and overcome. "Death, as never before," observed ethicist Robert Veatch in the mid-1970s, "is looked upon as an evil, and we are mobilizing technology in an all-out war against it. If not death itself, at least certain types of deaths are beginning to be seen as conquerable."[5]

With this shift in physicians' attitudes toward disease, death, and the practice of medicine, the paternalism characterized by an insistence that the doctor always knows best and by a reluctance to disclose terminal diagnoses suddenly took on a very different meaning—with drastically different consequences for the patient. Surveys conducted at hospitals during the 1950s revealed that as many as 90 percent of all physicians routinely failed to share a terminal diagnosis with their cancer patients,[6] and this at a time when more and more patients were being subjected to some form of resuscitation or life-sustaining treatment.

Withholding painful information from hopelessly ill patients (however misguided a policy) was one thing; routinely forcing treatment on patients who had not even been informed of their condition—much less the potential risks and benefits of treatment—was something else entirely. Predictably, the 1960s and 1970s witnessed a flurry of court cases in which patients successfully sued their physicians for failure to disclose information about their conditions and/or the options available for treatment.[7] These decisions not only reinforced the legal principle of informed consent in the age of medical high technology, but also precipitated a dramatic shift in physicians' attitudes and behavior. According to a 1978 poll, as many as 97 percent of physicians working with cancer patients preferred to inform their patients of a terminal diagnosis—certainly a remarkable shift in behavior during the twenty years since the earlier polls were taken.

By the mid-1970s, the legal principle of informed consent for terminally ill patients had been secured in court case after court case. With that right firmly in place for competent adult patients, the crucial legal issue became a patient's competence to choose or not, and to what extent to accept medical treatment. Since 1980, a variation of that issue has been the right of patients to be free of unwanted medical treatment, even if they are not, or never were, competent. By what criteria should caregivers evaluate patients' decision-making capacity? The way this question is settled has enormous significance for the way patients and potential patients can insure that their wishes will be honored should they become legally incompetent to speak for themselves.

Before we look at the question of competence, we should first point out a notable exception to the rights of competent adult patients to direct their own treatment: the special case of emergency medicine.

The requirement of informed consent is routinely suspended in emergency treatment situations, where the physician and other members of the emergency team are understandably "privileged" to forego consent during the critical moments in which life or death is determined. At the time of accidents and sudden illnesses, this suspension of a patient's right to choose is generally unavoidable, even unfortunately in those rare cases where the patient might not have desired the procedure. More questionable and potentially abusive practices began to surface in the late 1960s and early 1970s, as CPR became aggressively applied to almost all patients with heart failure, regardless of a patient's wishes or prognosis. In response to this, a policy of nonresuscitation was routinely applied to certain elderly, chronically ill, and terminally ill patients, at first "silently" (i.e., unofficially) and at the discretion of the attending physician. In recent years this practice has become more openly observed and monitored, and subject whenever possible to the control of the patient's expressed wishes for treatment, not simply the physician's judgment. Today many hospitals have explicit policies that require written do-not-resuscitate (DNR) orders to be signed by, and placed in the medical files of, patients who do not wish to be revived in the case of coronary failure. Those who sign such orders are not signing away their access to full supportive care or involvement in other treatment decisions.[8]

COMPETENCE AND SUBSTITUTED JUDGMENT

Who can competently make decisions about their own treatment? The answer is relatively simple. Any adults who can demonstrate an understanding of their condition, as well as the probable outcomes of treatment and nontreatment, are legally competent to act on their own behalf. "The law presumes every adult is competent," writes George Annas, a leading authority on laws affecting patients' rights.[9] The burden of proof is always on those who would challenge a patient's competence to make a rational, self-interested decision. Not surprisingly, physicians rarely challenge the competence of a patient who agrees with their recommendations for treatment. Quite often, though, the refusal of a potentially life-sustaining medical procedure strikes physicians as sufficient grounds for challenging a patient's legal competence. Nevertheless, recent court rulings have, without exception, stated the matter differently, consistently affirming the competent patient's right to refuse any medical treatment for any reason whatsoever, whether or not the patient's caregivers agree with the decision and even if the failure to receive treatment will likely result in the patient's death. Refusal of life-sustaining or death-forestalling treatment is never in and of itself sufficient legal grounds for questioning a patient's competence.

Basic guidelines have been established for substituted judgment and surrogate decision making in situations where the patient's incompetence can be reasonably determined and conceded, such as cases involving infants, children, and persons with severe mental impairment. Most states, with the notable exception of New York, permit substituted decision making on behalf of such patients by their next of kin or legal guardian, including decisions to forego life-sustaining medical treatment.

The issue that has occupied the central position for the patients' rights movement during the past two decades, however, is the problem of once-competent patients rendered permanently incompetent by injury or illness. How can a patient's wishes regarding treatment be adequately determined? In situations where no clear advance instruction has been provided, who should decide on the patient's behalf? And how, and under whose supervision, should these treatment decisions be made?

Before the *Cruzan* ruling, the most famous and influential case of an incompetent patient's right to forego life-sustaining treatment involved twenty-one-year-old Karen Ann Quinlan, who was admitted to a New Jersey hospital in a state of irreversible coma in April 1975. Following her admission to the hospital, Quinlan became dependent on both a respirator for breathing and a nasogastric feeding tube. Insisting that she would not wish to continue living under such conditions, Joseph Quinlan petitioned to be appointed his daughter's legal guardian for the purpose of having the respirator removed. Opposed by both Quinlan's attending physicians and the state attorney general, the request was subsequently refused by a trial court. But in May 1976, the New Jersey Supreme Court reversed the decision of the lower court, requiring that the attending physician remove the respirator. Karen Ann Quinlan lived for nine more years, breathing on her own.

The New Jersey Supreme Court came to its decision by balancing the patient's right to refuse treatment, based on a constitutionally guaranteed "right to privacy," against a number of potential state interests, the most compelling of which in this instance was the state's asserted interest in preserving life. The principle that the state's interest in preserving life "weakens and the individual's right to privacy grows as the degree of bodily invasion increases and the prognosis dims,"[10] prevailed, and the court ruled that Quinlan's right to privacy under the circumstances outweighed the state's interest in keeping her alive. The New Jersey Court also ruled that the patient's family could most practically and effectively provide "substituted judgement" on the patient's behalf, thus preventing the patient's loss of her right to privacy due to her incompetence. In addition, the New Jersey Court also pointed out that such a judgment was subject to various safeguards.

These two legal principles, important to the Quinlan decision, were handled somewhat differently in the U.S. Supreme Court's decision in the *Cruzan* case. First, the Supreme Court questioned the sufficiency of the rights to privacy and informed consent in cases involving the removal of life-sustaining treatment from an incompetent patient. Instead, the justices based their decision on a person's "liberty interest," as guaranteed by the due process clause of the Fourteenth Amendment.[11] Second, the Supreme Court upheld Missouri's standard of "clear and convincing" evidence in cases where the patient's wishes are not conclusively or sufficiently documented, while recognizing that other states, like New Jersey, may use the principle of substituted judgment under similar circumstances. As a result, in states such as Missouri, which require strict standards of evidence, patients without living wills, durable powers of attorney, or other state-recognized advance directives, can be kept alive indefinitely. And since, as the Supreme court held in *Cruzan*, "an incompetent person is not able to make an informed and voluntary choice to exercise a hypothetical right to refuse treatment or any other right,"[12] patients' rights are jeopardized by their failure to provide in advance clear and convincing evidence of their wishes regarding life-sustaining treatment.

In such cases, incompetent patients who have not completed advance directives for medical care become, for all practical purposes, wards of the state. "There is no automatic assurance that the views of close family members will necessarily be the same as the patient's would have been had she been confronted with the prospect of her situation while competent," explained Chief Justice William Rehnquist concerning the Court's decision. "All of the reasons previously discussed for allowing Missouri to require clear and convincing evidence of the patient's wishes lead us to conclude that the State may choose to defer only to those wishes, rather than confide the decision to close family members."[13]

Despite its different approach, the U.S. Supreme Court's decision in *Cruzan* does provide significant constitutional protection for patients and future patients who want to insure that their wishes for life-sustaining treatment will be honored. The Court clearly recognized the conditional right of competent adult patients to be free of unwanted medical treatment. It also recognized that this right survives the patient's subsequent inability to make medical decisions. Further, in her concurring opinion in the ruling, Justice Sandra Day O'Connor noted that the Court's decision "does not preclude a future determination that the Constitution requires the States to implement the decisions of a patient's duly appointed surrogate. Nor," she continued, "does it prevent States from developing other approaches for protecting an incompetent individual's liberty interest in refusing medical treatment."[14]

In other words, the U.S. Supreme Court essentially recognized the enforceability of living wills, durable powers of attorney and other advance directives as protected by constitutional law. It is reasonable to conclude that the Supreme Court has gone a long way toward solidifying rights previously recognized by many individual states and has established new law applicable in those states that have not addressed the issue of foregoing unwanted medical treatment.

LIVING WILLS AND
OTHER ADVANCE DIRECTIVES

The idea of an "advance directive" for health care first began to emerge in the late 1960s. At that time, many individuals, concerned that they not be forced to endure life-sustaining technology, wrote open letters to their families, friends, physicians, and clergy describing their wishes for end-of-life treatment. These letters, which came to be known as "living wills," were not meant primarily as legally binding documents. The intent was to communicate preferences and guide caregivers. However, most people who wrote living wills during the early years believed that their wishes would be honored. The combination of the legally recognized principles of bodily integrity and informed consent with a patient's written directive was thought to be a sufficient guarantee. (See appendix A for a sample living will.)

However, problems quickly arose. For one thing, the original documents were terribly imprecise, many stating simply that the patient wished to forego "heroic" or "extraordinary" treatments. What these terms meant to different individuals in different situations often required interpretation and proved confusing even to those physicians most sympathetic to their patients' intentions. Even more troubling was the simple fact that, since they had not been shown to be legally binding, living wills were sometimes ignored or disregarded by the patient's caregivers. For those physicians who wished to follow their patients' instructions for end-of-life treatment, living wills did in fact prove to be legally valid; no physician or other health-care provider has ever been successfully prosecuted for acting in accordance with a patient's written advance instructions to forego life-sustaining treatment. But, on the other hand, physicians who disagreed with their patients' wishes were not clearly legally obliged to comply with the instructions provided in a living will.[15]

In response to the initially uncertain legal status of living wills and the inadequacy of many patients' directions, most states have now passed laws not only sanctioning advanced medical directives but also providing guidelines for their preparation and criteria for their use. Many state laws clearly express their intent only to clarify and expand the rights of those explicitly eligible for coverage, and not "to impair or supersede any preexisting common-law legal rights or responsibilities that patients and practitioners may have with respect to the withholding or withdrawing of life-sustaining procedures."[16] But other living will laws are so narrowly written that they severely limit the medical conditions under which the living will can be honored. And some laws even limit the kinds of life-sustaining treatment a person can choose to forego. In the wake of the *Cruzan* decision, the constitutionality of state laws with such limitations is highly questionable.

DURABLE POWER
OF ATTORNEY

Most states have sought to expand further the rights of incompetent patients by recognizing by statute the right of competent adults to authorize someone to make medical decisions in the event that they become unable to make those decisions for themselves. It is generally referred to as a "durable health care power of attorney." The rights of the person authorized to make medical decisions under a durable power of attorney are generally the same as those of the person for whom the decisions are being made.

Laws regarding living wills and health care proxies of attorney vary from state to state, with some states having one or the other, some both, and some even combining the two on the same document. (See appendix A for a sample durable power of attorney document.) Regardless of a particular state's laws, it is always in the interest of the patient or future patient to combine both types of directive, even if one is not legislatively sanctioned by the state. Durable powers of attorney, by legally conferring on another person all the rights of the patient, circumvent many of the restrictions that often limit the rights of incompetent patients with only living wills, and they allow surrogates to make decisions about factors like unanticipated illness and new technology. Living wills, on the other hand, allow patients to clarify not only their decisions but also the thought processes and value systems behind those. An articulate surrogate who can speak forcefully on behalf of the patient's clearly documented values and wishes, and can adjust those wishes to circumstances that could not be anticipated, is most likely to inspire the confidence and cooperation of the patient's physicians and nurses.

Since the laws vary considerably from state to state, it is important that living wills and instructions to surrogates conform closely to the guidelines of the existing state laws. However, the writer may wish to go further by also providing guidelines for treatment that go beyond what is permitted by the statute (e.g., a rejection of artificial nutrition and hydration by a resident of a state whose law disallows cessation of artificial nutrition and hydration). If you do, however, go beyond the bounds of state law in completing a living will, you should specifically state that your choices for treatment are based on an understanding of and commitment to the common-law principles of bodily integrity, informed consent, and self-determination. Lawyers will point out that many existing advance directive statutes are flawed and in need of some amendment. However, the combination of a living will and an appointed proxy, together with a written appeal to the broadest possible interpretation of common and constitutional law, goes a long way toward ensuring that a patient's wishes will be honored.

NOTES

1. Robert M. Baird and Stuart E. Rosenbaum, eds., *Euthanasia: The Moral Issues* (Buffalo, N.Y.: Prometheus Books, 1989), 194.
2. Ibid., 181.
3. Robert M. Veatch, *Death, Dying, and the Biological Revolution* (New Haven and London: Yale University Press, 1989), 91.
4. President's Commission for the Study of Ethical Problems in Medicine and Biomedical Research, *Deciding to Forego Life-Sustaining Treatment* (Washington, D.C.: Government Printing Office, 1983), 51–52.
5. Veatch, *Death, Dying,* 3.
6. President's Commission, *Deciding to Forego,* 54.
7. George J. Annas, *The Rights of Patients* (Carbondale and Edwardsville: Southern Illinois University Press, 1989), 101 n. 7.
8. President's Commission, *Deciding to Forego,* 251.
9. Ibid., 89.

10. Baird and Rosenbaum, *Euthanasia*, 182.
11. Ibid., 183.
12. Ibid., 184.
13. Ibid., 188.
14. Ibid.
15. President's Commission, *Deciding to Forego*, 140–141.
16. Ibid., 144.

THREE

Medical Technology: Hope and Peril

... that nothing might be left undone on the margin of the impossible.
T. S. ELIOT
The Family Reunion

Mr. T., who is seventy-eight, has suffered from Alzheimer's disease for six years. He lives in a nursing home, where his wife visits him every day. Recently he has eaten very little and has been losing weight. He rejects the efforts of his wife or his nurses to spoon-feed him and becomes angry and agitated when they try. Because of the weight loss, the nursing home asks for permission to place a feeding tube in Mr. T.'s stomach so that he can be adequately fed. Mrs. T. gives her permission. When she returns the next day, she is horrified to find her husband tied down in his bed by both hands as well as with a chest-restraint device. He is desperately trying to free himself from these restraints and has lacerated his arms and nearly choked himself in the effort. The nurses tell Mrs. T. that they have asked the doctor to prescribe a tranquilizer for Mr. T. in order to calm him down. They say the restraints were necessary because Mr. T. pulled the feeding tube out of his nose three times the night before.

Such is the hope and the peril between which medical technology increasingly places patients, their family, their physician, and their nurses. One observer noted:

The patient's recovery will be watched not only by nurses but by electric eyes too. Sensing devices will constantly monitor his heart

19

rate, his temperature, his respiration rate, his electrocardiogram and the blood pressure both in his veins and his arteries. The nurses will not rouse the patient early in the morning to poke a glass thermometer between his gums and then spend much of the day checking up on his and the other patients' conditions. They will simply push a button at the console of their station to get as many readouts as they want. The patient will not have to hope that if he enters a crisis somebody may spot it.[1]

When this was written in 1966, it may have evoked images of a brave new medical world in which human ingenuity has been harnessed in a technological and scientifically predictable fashion in the interest of human health. As it continues, the passage underscores this emphatically: "If any single bodily function or combination of functions deviates beyond the fixed limits the patient's physician has programmed into a computer, lights will flash and a buzzer will sound the alarm. Within seconds, nurses, technicians, doctors and a complete array of equipment will be in action at his bedside."[2]

Since this was written at a time when medical technology was in its infancy, the tone of unqualified awe is perhaps understandable. With the passage of time and the benefit of over thirty years of experience, our sense of awe is now considerably more qualified. We continue to be amazed by the capacity technology places in our hands and the medical wonders we can achieve as a result. We cannot deny the progress we have made in treating certain diseases, extending life, and easing suffering. But as we have done away with most deaths from pneumonia, tuberculosis, and other chronic diseases, we have become increasingly likely to die from prolonged or chronic illnesses such as cancer or heart disease. New reservations that could not have been anticipated thirty years ago now temper our enthusiasm for the intensive use of medical technology, particularly in the final stages of terminal disease.

TREATMENT AT ALL COST

This wariness comes from firsthand experience. In a growing number of situations medical technology presents us with a harsh dilemma: whether to be a victim of disease or a prisoner of technology. Perhaps because of all that modern medicine can do for us when we are ill, we realize now more than ever that there is no substitute for good health. And when good health is absent, but death is not yet immediate, we are confronted by the problem of how far we, as physicians and patients, ought to go to control disease and how dependent on technology we are willing to become to achieve that.

In order to make these decisions responsibly, we must understand better how technology has transformed medical practice and how, in so doing, it might, if unchecked, tip the balance away from personal control over its use and toward impersonal systems dictating its use at any cost. The questions become as basic as, What is success in medical care? This is especially true in those clinical situations where technology allows medical and nursing staff to maintain the patient almost indefinitely somewhere between life and death. For now there is a practice of medicine that, to borrow from something T. S. Eliot wrote in a not-altogether-different context, can be pursued

> Not for the good that it will do
> But that nothing might be left undone
> On the margin of the impossible.[3]

Lewis Thomas, the noted physician and essayist, seems to have anticipated the problem facing us today when he coined the phrase "halfway technology,"[4]—that is, medical technology that neutralizes the effects of certain life-threatening diseases without actually healing the patient. Patients may be kept from dying, but also from living—if living is seen as including physical, emotional, or mental activity. Does a patient in a permanent "vegetative" state represent successful medical practice? If not, is it reasonable to pursue such practice? However, if the answer is no, we have the truly difficult task of determining the point beyond which practicing medicine in this way becomes inappropriate. Technology is everywhere in medical care today. On balance, that is seen as good, as long as the technology helps to heal and does not harm the patient. When neither condition is true, the presumption of technology's value no longer holds. At that point technological medical care has become intrusive.

Ethicist Joseph Fletcher defines technology as "the scientifically disciplined and sophisticated invention of devices to serve the ends or goals or 'goods' we cherish."[5] Applied to medicine, the goals served are health, life, and psychophysical well-being. Fletcher adds that medical technology is not just "hardware" but also "software," not just mechanical but also chemical, biological, physical, psychological, and surgical. As long as medical technology is applied to the ends of human health, we can presume that the technology is subordinated to patient interests as determined by the patient and the physician. However, there is a growing awareness that medical technology, like technologies in other settings, tends to dominate medical decisions unless patient, physician, and family work to keep it in a subordinate role. For example, the 1984 U.S. Congress Office of Technology Assessment (OTA) report on intensive care units describes the phenomenon known as the "technology treatment imperative."[6] In simple language, this means that the knowledge that something can be done for a patient creates an urgency to do it. As a consequence, physicians tend to provide life-support care, for example, long after any reasonable justification for it has ceased.

Diane Meier, an associate professor at Mt. Sinai School of Medicine, agrees that a technological treatment imperative exists. But she describes its effect in the clinical setting somewhat differently: "There is the pressure that because it exists, you better have a good reason to not use it."[7] In other words, as Meier explains it, the burden of proof—making very clear why an available technology is not to be used—rests with the physician. But so difficult is the process for proving to the satisfaction of regulatory agencies that a decision—for example, not to give antibiotics or not to insert a feeding tube—is clinically correct, that medical and nursing staff are inclined to follow the path of least resistance. This is particularly true in the nursing home setting.

While she understands the inclination, Meier believes it should be resisted. "I think doctors should go through that process. I think they should be willing to have their thinking scrutinized." To make such decisions, doctors must record their reasoning in the patient's chart and work with other members of the medical team to achieve wider agreement. Needless to say, this process complicates matters, requires considerable time, and brings no financial rewards. "So there are incentives for doctors not to go through this very time-consuming and agonizing process of deciding not to use technology. It's easier, faster, and cheaper just to use it."

The OTA report agrees. It argues that since decisions to withhold or withdraw life-sustaining treatment from patients in intensive care units are shared by a number of people, there is a tendency to succumb to the technological imperative to treat.[8]According to the report, other factors also contribute to this technological imperative. Among them are the moral distinctions characteristic of traditional medicine, which predispose physicians and nurses to provide more care than patients might otherwise request if they were in a position either to make their own decisions or to participate actively with medical and nursing staff in the decision-making process.[9]

Another factor is the threat of malpractice suits. Medical staff working in settings like the intensive care unit, where the care provided usually means the difference between life and death, must practice legally defensible medicine. First, there is a direct causal connection between radical medical decisions that are implemented and the radical medical outcomes that occur. For example, when the decision to withdraw artificial feeding and hydration is carried out, death by starvation and dehydration will follow as a direct result relatively quickly. Combined with the still-uncertain legal and regulatory environment in which such decisions are made, this connection leads to an imperative to treat. And as a result, "the legal, lawsuit environment and the regulatory environment, which were set up to protect patients, have the unintended side-effect of having a lot of people inappropriately treated." In these circumstances that means being treated when the medical indications call for no treatment because it would serve no medical purpose.

So far, the factors considered here as contributing to the technological imperative to treat have been extraneous to the medical technology itself. The OTA report, however, argues very clearly that something inherent in the nature of medical technology itself creates the conditions from which a technological imperative would naturally come.[10] In a much broader discussion of technology itself, Lewis Mumford, the noted educator and social critic,

explains why this is: "Not merely does technology claim priority
in human affairs; it places the demand for constant technological
change above any considerations of its own efficiency, its own
continuity, or even, ironically enough, its own capacity to survive."[11] Mumford adds something that may have particular
significance for the world of medicine: "To maintain such a system, whose postulates contradict those that underlie all living
organisms, it requires for self-protection absolute conformity by
the human community."[12] This raises two critical concerns for
Mumford. The first is the tension between technology and the
central, historic task of every man and woman—that of becoming
more human. The second, closely connected to the first, is the
observed tendency of technology's advocates not to want to bring
technology itself under constant human evaluation and direction.

REMEMBERING THE PATIENT

The issue for an individual patient and family comes down to the
threat of treatment for the sake of treatment. Medical technology
tends to "atomize" the patient, providing treatment system by
system, organ by organ. Even when medically "successful," the
results may contribute little to the patient's sense of well-being.
Cardiopulmonary resuscitation (CPR), for example, can reverse
cardiac arrest, even in the case of a patient suffering end-stage
(incurable) dementia. In such a case, the heart may have been
revived, but the patient is still demented. As far as the patient is
concerned, the fact that his or her heart is beating once more
probably has little significance.

Many doctors feel that the risks and benefits of technology have
meaning only within the context of the individual patient and his
or her expectations. For example, "a relatively vigorous seventy-
year-old, diagnosed with metastatic breast cancer, may choose
chemotherapy, even knowing the side effects and quality-of-life
costs of chemotherapy because, for one reason, she's pretty
healthy and is likely to survive the side effects, and for another, she
has a fifteen-to-twenty-year life expectancy if the breast cancer can
be brought under control," according to Meier.

With other contexts and expectations, the decision about chemotherapy may be very different, even if it promises to be just as successful as in the first case. "An eighty-seven-year-old with the same diagnosis, who may have other medical problems, such as severe arthritis or heart failure, might choose not to undergo chemotherapy. For one reason, her life expectancy is not that long, even in the absence of breast cancer, and for another, if you added this quality-of-life burden on top of the others, it would just be unbearable."

For doctors and their patients confronting life-threatening illness, the decisions grow increasingly complex. "The practice of medicine is harder because of the presence of the technology that's available to us. It means we have to think a lot more about what we are doing, and we have to do things less automatically than we used to," says Meier. Physicians trained thirty years ago did not have options like feeding tubes, ventilators, and intensive care units. Forced to fall back on their own innate resources, the most they could do was the best they could do. Frequently that was not enough. In stark contrast to physicians today, physicians earlier in this century did not have the luxury of considering to withhold or withdraw treatments. Physicians had little to offer against life-threatening illness, particularly before the availability of antibiotics. But things are very different today, since medical personnel can choose from a variety of measures, all extremely effective in prolonging human life. "Sometimes these tools prolong a life that's worth living; very often, they prolong a life that's not worth living to the individual who is subjected to their intervention."

What should be obvious by now is that half of the technological equation is missing—as far as the patient is concerned, the most important part. According to Meier, "One of the things that's most needed now is outcomes assessment of the different interventions in different age groups and in different disease processes." For many terminally ill patients no one is yet certain whether artificial nutrition and hydration will afford some acceptable level of human existence or will merely confine them to bed for the duration of their illness. In the face of this uncertainty, and in the absence of compelling data to the contrary, doctors and nurses will remain inclined to intervene with their medical technologies.

WHERE DOES TREATMENT LEAD?

To make a decision about a particular technology, it is important to understand that these mimic, but do not replace, the systems or organs of the body. In life-threatening illnesses, their purpose is short-term: to provide the support necessary until the patient's own ailing system or organ will recover sufficiently to resume its natural function. Take the case of a patient with an underlying and severe chronically obstructive lung disease who contracts pneumonia. As a result of the pneumonia, whatever capacity the patient's lungs had to breathe on their own becomes extremely limited, and the patient's life is threatened. Under these circumstances, a physician will now routinely decide to put the patient on a ventilator with the hope that when the pneumonia has responded sufficiently to the antibiotics, the lungs will be able to take over as before. That, in turn, will make it possible to remove the patient from the ventilator. In a medical crisis, the technology functions as a substitute, in this case for the lungs. But it is never intended to be a permanent substitute for the human biological system. "When physicians advise mechanical ventilation," notes Meier, "the hope is that the reversible process will be reversed and the patient will be able to do without the mechanical ventilation assistance until the next superimposed infection or other problem comes up."

Regrettably, that does not always happen. In such a case, both patient and physician face a substantially different clinical situation. In addition to chronic lung disease, there is now the possibility of chronic dependence on a ventilator as a condition of staying alive. For some patients, this may be an intolerable outcome. Others may wish even a slight chance for their lungs to recover. However, the decision to stop using the ventilator, to withdraw it, is of a different and even more complex order than the decision never to start it.

Other, more typical circumstances, particularly in the case of elderly patients, illustrate the same point. For example, a patient can stop breathing or suffer cardiac arrest for several possible reasons, such as a heart attack or an abnormality in the patient's blood chemistry. If this happens in a hospital or nursing home, the patient will normally be given CPR and placed on a ventilator. But there are many unknowns. It may not be clear, for example, whether the patient has suffered serious brain damage or if the damage to the heart is irreversible. Since that cannot be known immediately, the natural inclination of physicians and nurses is to resuscitate the patient, on the assumption that the damage is reversible. Then, the hope is that the technology, like a cast for a broken limb, can be withdrawn to allow the patient to function independently.

Here again, many sobering considerations confront us. If the patient is elderly, the chances of coming through the crisis, even with the technology, are slight. "If we see an eighty-two-year-old person have a cardiac arrest," says Meier, "we pump on his chest, give him medicine and put him on a ventilator, while recognizing the odds are very poor that the person is going to survive and be able to come off the ventilator and return to any kind of independent function." Despite those odds, however, and because there is still some chance for the patient to survive, physicians are inclined to proceed with treatment.

Any carefully written living will must take account of this deeply rooted inclination to treat. It is also important to understand what being supported by medical technology means physically and emotionally. For instance, when a patient is put on a respirator to assist his breathing, it requires a procedure known as intubation, which can be done in one of three ways. *Oral intubation* involves placing an endotracheal tube into the patient's windpipe through his mouth. Once in place in the windpipe, a soft rubber cuff is inflated, creating a kind of pressure chamber between the tube and the windpipe essential for an efficient flow of air. Externally, the tube is held in place by being taped to the side of the patient's mouth and then attached to the respirator. *Nasal intubation* involves passing the endotracheal tube through the patient's nose. Finally, a patient can be intubated by means of a *tracheostomy*. This is a surgical opening in the lower part of the neck through which the tube is inserted directly into the patient's windpipe.

While it is usually not painful to be on a respirator, it is not comfortable, either, certainly not over a prolonged period. Patients often become agitated and try to pull out the tube. The intubated patient is always sedated to some degree, or his or her hands are restrained with soft restraints, or both. This avoids the possibility of removing the tube and inflicting serious damage. Nasal intubation can lead to sinusitis and oral intubation makes oral hygiene very difficult. With a tracheostomy, which can be either temporary or permanent, the endotracheal tube has to be tied in to prevent any movement for the first two days. Because a tracheostomy is a surgical procedure, there is always the risk of infection, and if there is too much movement of the tube, bleeding can result. Patients who are intubated through the mouth cannot speak. Communication with family or the medical staff must be done with written messages.

The emotional effects of being attached to a ventilator are more serious. "If you take an elderly patient who has several illnesses and takes a number of medications before the cardiac arrest occurs or before he or she requires the ventilator, it is very common to see agitation, confusion, and delirium," notes Meier. It can be very distressing for an older person with an acute, life-threatening illness to wake up, for example, in an intensive care unit with hands tied and tube inserted in his or her windpipe.

Whether this is inhumane, even barbaric, is now hotly debated. Physicians and nurses justify it to the extent that it is, in their clinical judgment, necessary to protect the interests of their patients. It may indeed be a price worth paying under some medical circumstances, but that is for the patient to decide—something difficult to do without a clear understanding of the technologies themselves and without advance planning.

Other factors should enter into the decision. "Once a person requires ICU-like interventions, the number of complications and other problems they'll get, because they are in a vulnerable condition, is high." Meier points out, for example, that patients who contract pneumonia severe enough to require a ventilator and intensive care have high chances of falling victim to many other infections. First, the hospital environment, with its abundance of bacteria, poses its own risks. More specifically, these patients will have a catheter placed in the bladder, increasing their risk of bladder infections. The catheter can also be uncomfortable.

Intravenous lines or tubes placed in the patients' arms or possibly neck can also trigger complications. Effective and sophisticated as such technological interventions are, they still pose serious risks to the patient. "All these treatments, while they can be life-saving, also have major risks associated with them. So what happens physically is that one problem leads to another and then there's a cascadelike deterioration." Of course, there are exceptions, particularly in the case of older patients with more physical or emotional reserves than are usually found in critically ill people. According to Meier, these exceptions are the cases doctors remember and then use as models when they consider treating, or actually treat, other patients aggressively. For this very reason, patients who are facing the possibility of life-sustaining treatments should make sure that the physicians involved fully appreciate not only the previous illnesses but also the quality of life that they, these particular patients, enjoyed prior to the immediate crisis.

Perhaps the most controversial medical technology today is artificial nutrition and hydration. In the last ten years a number of ways of nourishing critically ill patients have become available. The most common is a nasogastric tube, a very soft plastic tube that is run through the nose into the esophagus and then into the stomach. This allows the passage of liquid food, which has the consistency of a milk shake and which contains the vitamins, minerals, and calories required to sustain a patient who cannot or will not eat. In the absence of other serious medical problems, and as long as they continue to breathe and have a functioning heart, patients can stay alive almost indefinitely with artificial feeding.

Like the ventilator, the nasogastric tube is not painful, but it can be uncomfortable. When it is being inserted, it tends to make the patient gag as it passes through the back of the throat. However, once the tube is in place, the gagging stops. Patients often develop a sore throat with a nasogastric tube. In addition, patients, who are feeling distressed or confused often try to remove what is obviously a foreign body taped to their face. When this happens, patients have their hands tied to prevent them from removing their only source of nourishment.

When inserting a nasogastric tube, the physician hopes, as with a ventilator, that the underlying problem preventing the patient from eating and drinking is reversible. Once the problem has been overcome, the assumption is that the technology can be removed and the patient can resume eating and drinking normally. "So, for example," says Meier, "when an Alzheimer's patient, who is at home and was eating, gets pneumonia, becomes agitated, and refuses to eat, a feeding tube will be inserted in order to help the patient through the acute pneumonia." Even with antibiotics, it is impossible to treat pneumonia successfully if the patient is malnourished. But with enough antibiotics and adequate nourishment, the medical hope is that the patient will get over the pneumonia, begin to eat again, and return home.

That may be the hope, but the reality may work out differently. "Often the acute pneumonia will not entirely resolve itself. That is, once an acute event like that occurs, the dementia process accelerates and the patient gets worse," notes Meier. Even if the pneumonia is successfully treated, the patient can fail to resume eating again. "As a result, at that point the physician, the patient, and the family are presented with the alternatives of continuing tube feeding or removing it and seeing the patient die from not eating and drinking."

If the inclination is to continue nourishment when the patient shows little interest—or indeed is refusing—the medical staff will probably consider a gastrostomy, that is, a small incision in the abdomen to insert a feeding tube through the stomach wall directly into the stomach. Much more comfortable than the nasogastric tube, the stomach tube can stay in place for a very long time without excessive inconvenience to the patient.

There are patients whose gastrointestinal tract is not working properly for reasons such as an inflamed bowel or major intestinal surgery. In those cases feeding is usually provided by inserting a catheter into a blood vessel, usually in the neck. A specially designed fluid is delivered directly into the bloodstream, containing all the required nutrients. This is known as "total parenteral nutrition" (TPN). It can be self-administered and is compatible with a reasonable level of independence, as long as the patient keeps meticulously clean the area where the catheter is inserted.

"Because we now have the ability to keep people from dying from not eating and drinking," Meier notes, "it's very hard for us not to use that technology even though [death by starvation or dehydration] may be the most easy and gentle death for many patients." Some hospice workers, for example, feel that death by dehydration is a very comfortable death, and clinical evidence supports that view, as long as dying patients receive medical care that keeps their mouth and lips moistened. There is also clinical evidence that both advanced age and neurological damage can diminish a person's sense of thirst and that under these conditions the body may produce its own pain-killing substances.[13] Dying by starvation takes longer, but also can be peaceful. Conscious patients generally slip into a coma near the end. Nurses and doctors, however, and particularly doctors, are often uncomfortable with such an outcome, simply because they have the means to prevent it.

As we consider our living wills and advance directives, we would do well to measure the advantages and disadvantages of medical technology against the ways we might die without it. If we can appreciate the pressures on the doctors and nurses who will care for us, while also clearly communicating our own desires, we can help to keep the genie of technology safely contained.

NOTES

1. Warren Young, "Bold Overhaul for Hospitals," *Life*, 2 December 1966, 110–111.
2. Ibid.
3. T. S. Eliot, *The Family Reunion*, in *The Complete Poems and Plays 1909–1950* (New York: Harcourt Brace Jovanovich, 1971), 237–238, pt. 1, sc. 1.
4. Lewis Thomas, "On the Science and Technology of Medicine," *Daedalus* 117 (Summer 1988): 303.
5. Joseph Fletcher, "Technological Devices in Medical Care," in *Who Shall Live? Medicine, Technology, Ethics,* ed. Kenneth Vaux (Philadelphia: Fortress Press, 1970), 117.
6. U.S. Congress Office of Technology Assessment, *Report on Intensive Care Units* (Washington, D.C.: Government Printing Office, 1984).
7. Diane Meier, interview with authors, February 1991. All subsequent quotations by Dr. Meier cited in this chapter are from this interview.
8. U.S. Congress, *Intensive Care Units.*
9. Ibid.
10. Ibid.
11. Lewis Mumford, *The Myth of the Machine* (New York: Harcourt Brace Jovanovich, 1970), 283.
12. Ibid.
13. Judith C. Ahronheim and Rose M. Gasner, "The Sloganism of Starvation," *The Lancet*, 3 February 1990.

FOUR

Making Our Wishes Known

In the face of death we can discriminate between the important and
the trivial. We sometimes drop our habitual or guardian reticence
and speak clearly.

LEWIS HYDE
The Gift

"The desire to have a death of one's own," wrote the poet Rainer
Maria Rilke shortly after the turn of the century, "is becoming
more and more rare. In a short time it will be as rare as a life of
one's own."[1] In those days, before the great advances in antibiotics
and medical technology, Rilke's was something of a lone voice
crying in the wilderness. Today, however, his remarks seem more
than prophetic. Eight out of ten of us will die in a tiny hospital
room, our perceptions clouded by tranquilizers and pain relievers,
most likely kept alive by one form of the technology described
thus far. Many of us will face our own death without ever having
witnessed firsthand the death of someone else, even those closest
to us. Yet none of this is by choice. Surveys indicate that, almost
without exception, we object to the denial, the anonymity, and the
loss of control.

BRINGING DEATH OUT OF HIDING

The attempt to change this situation began in the 1960s, when a
number of social movements and ethical traditions came together

to form the patients' rights movement. Associated with this effort to inform and empower patients was a new interest on the part of doctors, ethicists, historians, and medical sociologists in the modern science of thanatology, or the study of death and dying. Many then-current practices in the care of the terminally ill were placed in a larger historical context, revealing that they not only increased suffering and anxiety but were inconsistent with deeply held values and beliefs.

The innovative work of a number of therapists and psychologists, most notably Elizabeth Kübler-Ross, brought new insight into the way individuals face their own illnesses and death, as well as the loss of those they love. To Kübler-Ross and others, dying was seen as a rich, complex human experience, not simply the end result of a failed medical intervention.

As death was brought out of the closet and into acceptable discourse, a diversity of articles and beliefs brought new questions. For example, a growing interest in Eastern religion—particularly Zen and Tibetan Buddhism—during the same period brought for many the certainty that death is a natural part of the process of living, and not something to be feared or denied. As a result of such changes, many within Jewish and Christian communities began to look again at their own traditions regarding dying, death, and the appropriate role of medicine and technology.

As discussion became more open, people around the country, many of them concerned older citizens, began to challenge the life-at-all-costs mentality of prevailing medical practice. Some saw the use of sophisticated life-sustaining technology as an inhumane intrusion on a dying person's final experience. Advocates of a "natural death" worked to counter the use of unwanted, unnecessary medical interventions that interfered with and degraded the natural process of dying. The hospice system, which started in England, is an important outcome of this movement (see chapter 5 for more details).

A more radical perspective arose among "right-to-die" advocates who believe that patients should have not only the option to avoid unwanted treatment, but also the option to end their own lives as they become overwhelmed by the pain and indignities of dying. On the surface, the values and goals of the natural death and right-to-die movements appeared contradictory: one sought to abolish all "unnatural" interventions to the process of dying; the other demanded the option of a drastic, life-ending intervention to stop suffering and pain—perhaps the most "unnatural" intervention of all. In reality, however, these differences were often blurred. Both natural death and right-to-die advocates worked together for the common goal of patient autonomy and self-determination, through which patients could decide for themselves the preferred approach.

This newly public debate about death has had an overwhelming impact. Through the efforts of concerned citizens, lawmakers, and medical professionals, much has been done to empower patients to regain more and more control over the conditions in which they die. The natural death, death-with-dignity, and right-to-die movements have made many gains, and overwhelming popular support for the principles behind them has become evident. But such support has not translated into widespread action. Just as "everybody wants to go to heaven, but nobody wants to die," most of us wish to die with some degree of dignity and peace, but few of us are willing to take the steps necessary to make our wishes known. This resistance on the part of most of us, whatever the reasons, is a social problem that no court ruling, no state or federal laws, and no change in the behavior or policies of the medical profession can alter easily.

The only way to insure that our wishes are honored if we can no longer act on our own behalf is to make our wishes known in advance. Almost every state recognizes some form of advance directive or living will. Even in those where no specific provisions yet exist, principles of common and constitutional law make written directions and appointed surrogates a valuable influence on the process through which decisions will be made on one's behalf. And while it is unquestionably important that such documents be completed in advance, it is also important that we make equally certain that our family, friends, or whoever is appointed to make decisions on our behalf not only understand and be comfortable with our wishes and the reasons behind them, but also be prepared to speak forcefully and convincingly about our desires.

"The greatest value of the natural death acts is the impetus they provide for discussions between patients and practitioners about decisions to forego life-sustaining treatment."[2] In spite of the many faults and restrictions of current state laws, many crises at the end of life are avoided because of the exchanges of information and attitudes that routinely take place between patients and physicians while completing state-sanctioned documents. Avoiding the need for litigation and professional review—by reaching understandings before a medical crisis—is, and should be, the primary function of any law regarding natural death or the right to die.

The original intent of living wills, and the reason for the broad terms and imprecision of many of the early documents, was to facilitate open discussion among family members, friends, clergy, and physicians about the patient's or future patient's values, beliefs, and wishes regarding end-of-life treatment. No document or law can substitute for such discussion. Anyone who takes the necessary time and risks the potential anxiety involved in such discussions will benefit—in terms of both the likelihood that his or her wishes will be honored and the atmosphere in which treatment will be provided.

Acknowledging to ourselves, our family, and our friends the inevitability of our own death is often a difficult and demanding process. But we need to remember that denying reality will *also* affect our lives, as well as the lives of our loved ones and our caregivers. Preparing for death is not giving up. On the contrary, it is a way of taking control—perhaps the most important way we now have available. "I believe that to talk of accepting death when its approach is inevitable," writes Dr. Cicely Saunders, the founder of the modern hospice movement, "is not mere resignation or submission on the part of the patient, nor defeat or neglect on the part of the doctor; for each of them accepting death's coming is the very opposite of doing nothing."[3]

DISCUSSING DEATH WITH YOUR DOCTOR

Doctors, who train for up to a decade in the sciences of diagnosing and treating disease, have little preparation in caring for those to whom technology and medical treatments offer little or no hope of recovery. Many doctors are aware of this lack, and some of the most far reaching criticism of the medical profession's inability to confront the experiences and meet the needs of dying patients has come from within the profession itself.

All of us have been affected by changes in medical practices over the last several decades. For example:

> Whereas only 50 years ago it was the rare household that had not been touched by death, today many students in professional training have not previously been exposed to a dying person. Even medical students and residents are likely during their years of clinical training to miss the chance to attend for any length of time a patient in the shadow of impending death. Indeed many physicians and nurses have never stayed with a dying patient through the final few hours and have never actually seen a patient die except in an unsuccessful resuscitation attempt.[4]

Not surprisingly, this lack of familiarity with, and the avoidance of, death by physicians and other health-care providers diminish the quality of care received by dying patients. With little or no firsthand knowledge of the feelings and wishes of those near the end of life, physicians have often resorted to treating and communicating with patients in outdated or simply wrongheaded ways.

As we saw in chapter 2, even in the 1960s, more than 90 percent of all physicians were reluctant to inform their patients that they were dying, fearful that the news would cause them to lose hope and die more quickly.[5] This was especially true of cancer patients. As a result, many dying people were deprived of the opportunity to share in decisions regarding their treatment, to set their personal affairs in order, and to speak openly with those they loved. Another horrible side effect of this practice was that many patients, in such an atmosphere of pervasive deception and evasion, became falsely convinced that they were dying. "This problem can be complicated," writes David Hendin in *Death as a Fact of Life*, "if the person's illness calls for medical procedures that seem to be unusual or life threatening. Persuading such a patient that he is going to recover may be especially difficult when he has watched doctors and nurses deliberately deceive other patients who were actually dying."[6]

Unfortunately, the change in this policy was brought about in

the courtroom, not at the bedside. As the patients' rights movement began to gain momentum in the early 1970s and health-care
cases slowly crowded the courts, many physicians, fearing review
or litigation, understandably became much more willing to talk
with terminal patients about their conditions, despite their mis-
givings about what effect this information would have. As this
new openness became more widespread, the old "death-sentence
theory" of patient disclosure was abandoned. Upon learning of
their condition, terminal patients didn't simply give in to despair
and die; many actually lived longer and more fully than expected,
because they felt relieved from the anxious uncertainty about their
situation, could share in the control of their final treatment, and
could take comfort from the open support of family and friends.
In fact, most patients (as many as three out of four, according to
one study) reported that they already suspected the worst because
of the way those caring for them became distant and evaded their
questions.[7]

By the early 1980s, in a complete reversal of the situation
reported twenty years earlier, the great majority of physicians had
become willing to discuss a terminal diagnosis with their patients.
Increasingly, this change in the way doctors deal with dying patients has become a matter of principle for effective patient care,
not simply a reluctant compliance with policy or law. However,
a desire to be honest does not always translate into skill in doing
so. Physicians, like the rest of us, are sometimes clumsy and
ineffective when sharing bad news with their patients; patients
and family members frequently complain of the coldness and
indifference of doctors. Also, this willingness to discuss a terminal
diagnosis does not always mean a willingness to discuss and share
responsibility in options for treatment, nor is it an invitation to the
patient to take control of, or even become a partner in, the treatment decision-making process.

In this changing climate of doctor–patient relationships, what
can the patient do to improve communication? One very important thing to remember from the start is that many doctors—even
those committed to honoring their patients' wishes—are hesitant
to bring up the issue of death and terminal care. Rightly or
wrongly, physicians often feel that initiating such discussions will

cause their patients undue anxiety and fear. Many doctors insist that patients may feel, in spite of all assurances to the contrary, that the doctor suspects some serious risk of illness and that this is what has precipitated the discussion. Others are concerned that the topic itself may be such a source of unanticipated anxiety and discomfort that it will cause patients to withdraw from the physician and withhold information important for their continuing care.

Nevertheless, many of these same physicians welcome the questions, suggestions, and direction of their clients—*when the patient makes the first move.* And even those who are normally reluctant to involve their patients in certain stages of the decision-making process are likely to give far greater and more serious attention to the wishes of those who initiate discussions about terminal care *before* a diagnosis has been made or the serious stage of an illness has begun.

In order to bring up these issues in advance, each of us must develop a long-standing relationship with a personal physician with whom we feel comfortable. Many problems can hinder the cultivation of such a relationship—especially poor or inadequate planning; injury or illness that occurs while traveling away from home; and, as many in our society are so painfully aware, the simple lack of money or available services. For individuals without a regular physician, the discussion of advance directives often has to begin at the time of initial treatment or admission to a hospital, thus taking place in a much more direct and compressed fashion. But regardless of the situation, it is crucial that patients *not* wait for their physicians to make the first move in discussing advance directives. These discussions are both our right and our responsibility as patients, and in most cases it will continue to be necessary for us to initiate them.

As we will see in chapter 5, you need to be prepared to discuss a number of topics with regard to care at the end of your life. First, you and your physician should jointly examine your medical history in detail. Although no one can predict with certainty how or when a person will become ill, this will give your doctor the opportunity to explain the types of illnesses from which you will most likely suffer, the manner in which such illnesses normally progress, and the various options for treatment that are available.

It is also important that the two of you discuss any relevant values, beliefs, and commitments that influence your attitudes toward end-of-life treatment. Your physician should understand and accept not only your wishes but the reasons behind them. This will empower him or her to serve as your advocate when you enter a hospital or nursing home. It will also help your doctor identify and suggest specialists, as needed, who will be sympathetic to your outlook. Most importantly, it will help the doctor apply your point of view in specific crises that the two of you cannot yet anticipate.

In addition, you need to know something about your physician's values and professional commitments, as well as the policies of the institutions through which he or she will most likely provide your care. If there are any personal, professional, or institutional factors that might inhibit your wishes being honored by this physician, it is crucial that you know them *in advance,* before a crisis occurs. You may then be able to transfer your care to persons and institutions more sympathetic to your desires. Physicians who are themselves unable or unwilling to honor your wishes will often assist you in making such arrangements.

During these advance discussions, your physician will also be able to inform you of any existing laws or court rulings that might inhibit or forbid your desires. Regardless of your response to or attitude toward the law, it is important that you know of and become familiar with such obstacles *before* you, or those you love, must face a critical decision.

Finally, it is advisable that you inform your physician in advance regarding any other persons whom you have authorized to make treatment decisions on your behalf if you cannot decide for yourself. Whether you identify a family member, a friend, or a member of the clergy, your physician will have much greater confidence in and respect for other such decision makers at your bedside if he or she already expects to encounter them there.

Any official documents indicating such proxy decisions, as well as your living will, should, of course, be given directly to your physician following your initial discussions. Such documents will then become part of your ongoing medical file, and these will guide the decisions and actions of other caregivers if and when your own personal physician is not available.

DISCUSSING DEATH WITH YOUR MINISTER, PRIEST, OR RABBI

Religious beliefs and values strongly influence how we think about death. Speaking of the values that affect the way people plan for the end of life, William Nelson, the director of chaplaincy at the Veterans Administration Hospital in White River Junction, Vermont, points out that "for many of us, the basis of those values are spiritual beliefs and the questions that they answer for us: What is the purpose in my life? What gives my life direction and meaning?"[8]

Members of the professional clergy—ministers, priests, and rabbis—can play a special role in helping patients clarify and communicate their own values. Nelson points out a number of ways in which members of the clergy are suited to help patients and future patients as they begin the process of advance planning for terminal care.

First, the clergy can clarify for people the beliefs and doctrines of their own traditions. "Religious people need to have a sense of what their own tradition espouses about the actions or instructions regarding treatment that they are considering," says Nelson. Many people are inhibited from actually considering certain treatment options by misunderstandings of the beliefs and practices of their traditions. (See chapter 8 for a more detailed discussion.) By communicating with someone trained in theology, people can become better able to interpret their own wishes in a manner consistent with their religious tradition. Such a reconciliation of personal conviction and religious teaching enables many patients to be both more articulate in expressing their wishes for end-of-life treatment and more insistent in directing the fulfillment of those wishes.

Many people also seek out the clergy for help with counseling and self-reflection. Also, when conflicts and crises arise during the course of illness, patients and family members often turn to the

clergy to be their advocates and speak up for them to those
providing their care.

Unfortunately, clergy today too often assume only a marginal
involvement in planning for terminal care. According to Nelson,
this is usually the result of breakdowns in communication between patients, family, physicians, and the clergy themselves. "I
don't think it works nearly as well as it should," says Nelson,
speaking of the working relationship between physicians and the
clergy. "Physicians have a lot of respect for the clergy but often
don't really know how to use them or relate to them. There's a
general lack of understanding of what the clergy can and should
do in these situations—be a useful ally in support of the patient."

All too often, ministers, priests, and rabbis do not fully appreciate how important a role they can play in planning for death.
"Many times they're simply reluctant to bring it up to their pa-
rishioners," explains Nelson. "Clergy, like physicians, often feel
that people don't want to talk about these things. To understand
a healthy, productive relationship among patients and family,
physicians and clergy, think of each group as one of the three
points of a triangle. Generally there are only dotted points of
connectedness between the points because the communication is
often very superficial. I would argue for very solid lines with more
open, serious, spirited dialogue between patients and clergy, and
clergy with physicians on behalf of patients."

As with doctors, this situation leaves the responsibility for in-
troducing discussions of advance planning and end-of-life options
and for improving the relationship between physician and clergy
with each individual. "One thing you can do," Nelson points out,
"is to tell both parties in advance that copies of your living will or
durable power of attorney have been given to each of them. If
some question comes up later on and the minister steps forward,
the physician will already know that the patient had felt strongly
enough about [his or her] importance . . . to request his or her
involvement in the decision-making process."

Another thing we can do to facilitate the clergy–physician relationship is to encourage these professionals to meet and discuss
our advance directive and their plan for working together in case
of a crisis. In this way, problems regarding confidentiality and
visitation can often be worked out beforehand.

The clergy can also be especially helpful in resolving family conflicts and communication problems. Many people involved in advance planning or confronted with a treatment decision feel awkward or frightened in bringing up issues, or handling conflicts, with family and friends of the patient. Nelson points out that it's often easier for the patient or the doctor to ask a member of the clergy to arrange a meeting among those concerned. "By organizing these kinds of family meetings, clergy are often able to prevent moral dilemmas and family conflicts from happening simply by allowing family members to explain to one another in advance how they feel about the issues under discussion, and exactly what they would and would not want in a medical emergency."

For those not formally affiliated with any congregation, synagogue, or other religious group, chaplains are usually on staff at hospitals and other institutions to provide the same type of ministry and care as parish clergy. According to Nelson, "Chaplains will introduce themselves to the patient and announce their availability. Most of the time, they will excuse themselves from serving those patients with parish connections, except to let the patient know that they're available if needed. The last thing a chaplain wants to do is to break into established relationships, which are so important to the decision-making process." Consequently, chaplains routinely serve patients with no institutional membership who specifically request their assistance. Chaplains are also on hand in many emergency situations, or whenever end-of-life treatment options are considered and ethical questions weighed. "In my hospital," explains Nelson, "whenever questions of advance directives or end-of-life options are brought up, nurses generally say, 'Would you like to talk with a chaplain?' "

DISCUSSING DEATH
WITH FAMILY AND FRIENDS

As important as it is to maintain open communication with our physician and a member of the clergy, it is even more vital to engage in thorough and sensitive advance communication with our families and close friends. If we become bedridden or institutionalized, these are, after all, the people on whom we will depend most for emotional support and routine care. And when any of us loses consciousness or is otherwise rendered incompetent to make decisions, family and friends are the ones who will be consulted about our wishes for treatment or nontreatment— and in some cases, asked to decide in our place. Therefore, our family and close friends must have as clear and complete a knowledge of our beliefs, values, and wishes as possible, and they must be as comfortable and articulate as possible both in supporting our decisions and in speaking on our behalf.

Advance directives and the discussions they require can help avert the kind of family crises that often erode the confidence and cooperation of doctors, nurses, and hospital administrators. All too often, the conflicts that push treatment decisions into ethics committees, courts, and other systems of institutional review take place among family members, not between the doctor and patient. It is not unusual for patients who are still actively involved in the decision-making process to find their competence challenged by family unprepared for, or unable to accept, their wish to discontinue life-sustaining treatment. Sometimes the accuracy or authenticity of living wills or other medical directives is contested by family members or close friends who have not been thoroughly briefed as to both the patient's wishes and the values on which those were based. Caregivers are rightly confused by this type of crisis; and in cases where the patient has become incompetent, they are often understandably reluctant to choose between the conflicting opinions of friends and family members.

Almost all such conflicts could be avoided in most cases simply by discussing your wishes in advance with the important people in your life. According to Dr. James A. Booher, Chief of the Medical Staff and Chairman of the Bioethics Committee at Palm Beach Gardens Medical Center in Palm Beach Gardens, Florida, the importance of advance communication among family members has not lessened, even with the enactment of natural death legislation. "There are loads of organizations with different philosophical and ethical bases for making end-of-life treatment decisions," insists Dr. Booher, "but those of us on the front lines— whether we're involved in patient care, sitting on ethics committees, or working as administrators—are generally not philosophers. Usually, the best principle that we can apply in making decisions is, 'Do unto others what they would have you do unto them.' But what the patient would actually want in a particular situation is often very hard to decipher from the available evidence and the testimony of those who speak on the patient's behalf.[9]

"Even with our state's new patients' self-determination act," continues Dr. Booher, "which is provided to each client upon admission to the hospital, there is simply no way to anticipate every situation that may arise during the course of a person's illness, and how the patient would have us respond to it. I just don't think there is any way to codify problems of interpretation when it comes to acting on behalf of a terminally ill patient; there are always going to be questions. That is why it's so important that patients discuss with their family, thoroughly and in advance, not only the treatments they do or don't want in the event they become incompetent to choose for themselves, but the reasons they feel that way. This is often the best guide we have in making difficult and complex decisions."

In cases where individuals disagree with their family and friends regarding an anticipated treatment decision, advance planning gives everyone the opportunity to discuss and perhaps resolve their differences outside of the tension and stress of a hospital or emergency situation. And in those fairly rare cases in which differences of values and opinions are deeply rooted and no consensus is possible, advance planning at least gives family and friends adequate time to accept the finality of the patient's decisions. While it is difficult to accept treatment decisions at the end of life that in some way conflict with your needs or deepest beliefs, it is even more traumatic to discover and be forced to accept such decisions at the last minute, just as treatment is about to be refused or withdrawn.

NOTES

1. Rainer Maria Rilke, *The Notebooks of Malte Laurids Brigge,* trans. Stephen Mitchell (New York: Vintage Books, 1985), 9.
2. President's Commission for the Study of Ethical Problems in Medicine and Biomedical Research, *Deciding to Forego Life-Sustaining Treatment* (Washington, D.C.: Government Printing Office, 1983), 145.

3. Cicely Saunders, quoted in David Hendin, *Death as a Fact of Life* (New York and London: W. W. Norton, 1984), 114.

4. President's Commission, *Deciding to Forego,* 59–60.

5. Ibid., 53.

6. Hendin, *Death as a Fact,* 133.

7. President's Commission, *Deciding to Forego,* 54.

8. William Nelson, interview with authors, April 1991. All subsequent quotations from Dr. Nelson are from this interview.

9. James A. Booher, interview with authors, January 1992. All susequent quotations from Dr. Booher are from this interview.

FIVE

Putting a
Living Will to Work

He searched for his accustomed fear of death and could not find it.
LEO TOLSTOY
The Death of Ivan Ilyich

The ideal place for a thorough discussion, in advance of terminal
care, is in the doctor's private office. "It's vastly more comfortable . . . in the context of a primary care relationship in my office
than to wait until the patient is really sick," says Molly Cooke,
M.D., an associate professor of clinical medicine at the University
of California, San Francisco, and an attending physician at San
Francisco General Hospital. "It used to be, quite honestly, that I
tended, like most other doctors, to wait until I was dealing with
inpatients who had a really bad diagnosis, typically cancer or
AIDS, before I would bring advance directives up." Now Cooke
talks to about half of her patients about their medical preferences
during the course of routine office visits.[1]

In this setting, there may be twenty minutes at the physician's
disposal. The patient is feeling well and is probably there for the
sole purpose of renewing his or her medication. "So I may say,
'We have a little extra time today, and that gives me the chance to
talk to you about some things that are clearly not immediately
pressing questions but about which I would like to know your
thoughts. Then, if the time ever comes when together we're faced
with these questions, I'll know what you think.' "

Cooke finds this approach appealing because it allows her to

47

deal with the issues involved in terminal illness while her patients
are outpatients. There is a psychological advantage to this. "They
are dressed in their own clothes, and since they are not acutely
symptomatic, they're not focused on the medical problem at hand.
As a result, they can often be a little more reflective." Cooke finds
that her patients, when approached this way, usually want to go
home to talk things over with their spouse and other members of
the family. "And I think that they may just be overall more
autonomous."

When preferences for medical treatments at some point in the
future are being considered, it is critically important for the patient to feel in control. At the same time, when the physician–
patient relationship has some continuity, the physician can play a
positive role in properly informing those preferences. The importance of the psychological climate becomes clearer if one considers
a very different setting. "The polar opposite situation for me,"
points out Cooke, "is when I'm an attending physician on a ward
and the house staff say to me when I come in in the morning, 'We
admitted somebody last night who is terribly sick. We want you
to have a do-not-resuscitate (DNR) discussion with him.' "
In complying with standard hospital practice for the attending
physician to write the no-code or do-not-resuscitate order, both
doctor and patient are placed at a serious disadvantage. The
doctor must immediately, before the possibility of any kind of
personal rapport, ask an unknown patient whether he or she
would want to be resuscitated. The patient must cope with the
disturbing question of whether the doctor's main priority is to
determine what treatments to withhold, rather than ways to make
the patient feel better. Almost anything would seem preferable to
a practice like this, which can only arouse the anxiety of everyone
involved.

This realization has prompted the search for different ways to
identify patients' preferences for treatment at the end of life. "Discussing these with patients that I've known over time during
outpatients visits, where we have fewer symptoms than average,
feels much more comfortable to me. We've established during this
period that I will be as energetic as the clinical situation requires
and as [long] the patient wants me to help him get better." In
these circumstances, there is little reason for the patient to ques-

tion the sincerity of a physician's determination to act in his or her best interest. "For this reason," says Cooke, "I'd much rather have that discussion before we need to than wait until we have to have it under what I would consider quite adverse circumstances."

In the less urgent setting of the doctor's office, both patient and physician can begin what should continue to be an exploratory conversation. There is nothing binding about what is being said. Indeed, the doctor should always be alert for any change of mind. And the patient remains free to say that his or her preferences for treatment have changed during the course of this open-ended, ongoing conversation. "I have found that these conversations can be wonderful. People will, quite easily, start telling you what's really important to them in their life. And I've found with some regularity that I'm a lot closer to these people after we've had a treatment-preference discussion."

As an example, Cooke recalls the case of one patient whom she had treated for about twelve years. A woman in her sixties, the patient was being treated only for hypertension. Apart from that condition, nothing else about her health would have occasioned a discussion about a living will. During one office visit, since there was time available, Cooke broached the topic. Her patient's response was positive and frank. She proceeded to explain what was really important to her in her life, and using those values as her guide, stated clearly what her preferences for treatment were. "It was a lovely conversation," Cooke says. Afterward, the patient talked to her sister. "She went to her sister's for Thanksgiving, and I think my fantasy is that at the Thanksgiving table she brought up this whole issue." Later the patient called Cooke to tell her about the conversation, pointing out that many of the other people at the table had later raised the issue of an advance directive and treatment preferences with their own doctors. "It doesn't have to be a negative experience at all," notes Cooke.

Nevertheless, as we saw earlier, many physicians are extremely reluctant to have these kinds of discussions for fear that they would seriously threaten the relationship they want to have with patients. Two things may make a positive, rather than a negative, response from patients possible here. In her conversation, Cooke is explicit in saying that she has seen nothing wrong with the patient that has prompted the conversation. But she also points out that often, given the nature of the potential situations being discussed, it is difficult, if not impossible, to anticipate problems. "This is something that makes perfect sense to people."

In contrast, when the doctor has to bring up the issue of treatment preferences with acutely sick, hospitalized strangers, conversation makes patients confront the critical nature of their illness. That can have an unnecessarily painful effect on the patient. "People often need a certain amount of time to assimilate how sick they are." Unfortunately, that process sometimes has to be compressed, with distressing results. Cooke gives an example of a situation with which she is quite familiar: "Someone came into the emergency room because of a slight cough, but thinking he was basically fine, and then discovered, all in the space of three hours, that he is so sick with AIDS that the doctors are concerned he may die before he leaves the hospital."

Under these circumstances, the discussion of treatment preferences can be very uncomfortable. Inevitably, it makes patients confront the gravity of their illnesses at the same time that they are probably functioning, psychologically, at the level of denial. It is not surprising then that many physicians working with patients whose prognosis is bad refuse to discuss their treatment preferences, in order to avoid the suspicion that they want an excuse for not providing the best treatment available. Even here, however, a careful explanation has advantages. "You can't give the best possible care if you don't know what the patient's preferences are," says Cooke. "But even under these circumstances, you can deal with the anxieties patients have about what this discussion means regarding their physician's commitment to giving them the best possible treatment."

One of the ways to lessen a patient's discomfort with the discussion of treatment preferences and advance directives is to make it so routine that it is equivalent to asking the patient what his or her social security number is. However, these discussions should not be hasty or superficial. Cooke sees a perfunctory discussion as inadequate. "Since what I am really interested in is knowing how the patient makes the decision, I think it will always require a considerable degree of attention from all parties in the discussion." For Cooke, that means attentive, thoughtful, and sensitive listening and questioning by both the physician and the patient.

"I don't think you can get around the inherent importance of the discussion. I don't think that a real discussion can be done with a checklist, in the admitting area of a hospital, for example." So even though she approves of the efforts to make these discussions possible for every patient, Cooke doubts that they can be held effectively if no relationship with the patient exists.

Since most living wills and other advance directives will eventually be put to use in a medical setting, such as a hospital, it seems important to consider how knowledgeable people are of these settings. How important is it that they have a realistic grasp of the environment in which their advance directive will be operating? Cooke, for example, has some patients who have spent probably two hundred hours in any year being treated in hospitals, including intensive care units, or visiting sick friends in similar settings. As a result, they have extensive experience with hospital procedures, and some fully appreciate the importance of the relationship between attending physicians and consulting specialists. However, Cooke also deals with patients so unfamiliar with the medical setting that she must explain the possibility of another physician caring for them when a life-threatening condition arises. "I think that some people still think of medicine in terms of the village doctor and that they'll be taken care of by somebody who buried their mothers, delivered their children, and has known their family for twenty-five years."

A physician can help a patient understand the different types of treatment options in different situations. For example, procedures intended to sustain life differ from routine "palliative care," or treatment intended to relieve pain and make the patient comfortable. Because of this important distinction, vague advance requests for "no treatment at all" are not likely to be taken seriously by even the most sympathetic caregiver. After a patient has become incompetent, most physicians encountering a document that says nothing more than this would reason, usually correctly, that the patient did not realize what he or she was requesting. The majority of individuals who choose to forego life-sustaining treatment do not intend to give up access to basic palliative care.

Related to an appreciation of the medical setting is the patient's understanding of life-sustaining procedures. How well, for example, does the typical person understand what is involved in being attached to a feeding tube? (See chapter 3.) In all probability, not well at all. Cooke, reflecting on her experience, observes that many doctors have subtly discouraged their patients from requesting more extensive treatments. For example, a doctor who generally favors limited intervention may ask a patient whether he or she would want to be intubated. If the patient thinks so, the doctor might then take the patient to an intensive care unit. "I think that's manipulative, at least in the situations I have in mind where the 'field trip' is intended to change the patient's mind."

For someone unfamiliar with modern medical technology, just seeing an intubated person for the first time can be daunting. Therefore, using the patient's immediate reaction as the basis for a particular treatment preference would be most unreliable. "So I think the visual impact alone may not really increase the validity of the patient's preferences," says Cooke. Here much depends on the purpose behind giving patients a firsthand experience of technical procedures and clinical care settings. "If the intent of that is to increase the validity of the decisions they make, then it's great. But a lot of times, that's not why doctors do it."

As Cooke points out, there are people who, at the end of their life, having had extremely burdensome treatment, say that they would do it again, without hesitation. On the other hand, some people are terribly averse to being dependent on machines and to being in a technologically oriented environment unsympathetic to holistic values. "So you need to know how sophisticated people are about the nature of the treatments that are being anticipated. But you also have to know how much they *care* about what the treatments are like."

A living will can play a very important role here by fostering discussion between the patient-to-be and someone else who will be able, as a result, to explain and expand on the patient's point of view. "This is not to say that the document itself doesn't have independent value and validity. Clearly, it does." Nevertheless, when faced with patients unable to speak for themselves, physicians often question a document's validity because they doubt that the patient could have clearly imagined the actual situation or something similar.

For this reason, doctors prefer to see advance directives like living wills supplemented by the participation of a person named by the patient as a "proxy decision maker." Ideally, such a person will have discussed with the patient not only specifics regarding pain control or antibiotics, for example, but also the patient's feelings for what would be appropriate or inappropriate treatment. "I think," says Cooke, "the physician feels much better if he or she can talk to a person, and so I feel an essential purpose of a durable power of attorney is to promote discussion between the prospective patient and the proxy. Completing a written form is a great occasion to start that discussion."

When they are dealing with advance directives, many physicians are less interested in clinical details than statements of values. Cooke is one of those. Consequently, when she is discussing possible clinical eventualities with her patients and they express a particular treatment preference, she believes it is important to know the underlying reasons. One might be a concern over being dependent. Another might be the consideration of short- or long-term prognoses. "People are tremendously variable in terms of their sensitivity. And some people are gamblers in the sense that they will tolerate a lot of short-term burdens for even a small chance of a very good outcome." It is not easy for doctors to know those differences in people, even when they are close friends, unless they have asked, "When you said you want to be ventilated, why did you say that? What were you thinking about? What did you consider to be the benefits and the burdens there? How did you end up weighing them so as to arrive at your particular decision?"

Cooke sees another use to pressing for the reasons behind statements of preference. The physician might ask patients to imagine a clinical situation and then ask what their treatment preferences would be in that situation. Frequently, the response is, "I don't know." That could stop any discussion dead in its tracks if the physician's only purpose is to get an answer about specific preferences. But if the physician is also trying to discover a patient's values, he or she can simply go on to ask why it is hard to identify a preference. "What considerations are offsetting each other and making it hard to come to a decision?" asks Cooke. She recognizes that drawbacks exist in applying what a patient says in a somewhat theoretical discussion in the doctor's office to the actual situation, when it happens. "But I think you're safer generalizing if you have a sense of the values than if you just have the person saying, 'I'd want to be intubated.' "

Coming from a physician who has given much time and thought to establishing an effective patient–physician relationship regarding treatment preferences at the end of life, this is a very important observation. It is very hard for the physician to know whether, when people present their preferences in categorical ways—"I want everything done" or "I don't want anything done"—they want them to apply in every single instance. Cooke explains this in relation to some of her older patients who have a slowly progressive, but ultimately lethal, problem such as congestive heart failure or cancer. But a much younger group is also included, such as HIV-infected patients. Many times these patients will say that they do not want anything done. "But they hardly ever mean—really mean—'I don't want anything done.' And I think pressing beyond that simple clinical directive to what comes to you as you think about how you make this decision is really useful."

IN THE HOSPITAL OR NURSING HOME

When it is time to use them, advance medical directives are most likely to come into effect in a hospital or nursing home. As a result, people need to know how such institutions approach the issue of advance directives and incorporate the directives into daily procedures.

As the vice-president for medical affairs at Central Maine Medical Center, Laird Covey recognizes that hospitals have a substantial and growing stake in advance medical directives—because of state law, hospitals' internal policies and procedures, and relations between hospital patients and their medical and nursing staff. Assuming that most hospitals support the use of advance directives and wish to cooperate in their execution, Covey believes that people should prepare such documents with a clearer understanding of what is at stake for hospitals.

In practical terms, that entails a number of things. "One would be the importance of familiarity with the legislation that guides the advance directives in a particular state. Although there's good reciprocity [between states] in general, it helps to understand the variations that exist from one place to another," says Covey.[2] In a very mobile society, people in life-threatening medical situations do not necessarily find themselves admitted to a hospital in their home state. As a result, hospitals find themselves dealing with advance directives that originated in another state and that, in some details, may conflict with the hospital's own state law. This is particularly true of provisions relating to artificial nutrition and hydration. In light of the possibility of finding themselves in a hospital in another state, people should develop their advance directives so that hospitals will have as much flexibility as possible to act according to the patients' treatment preferences. (See appendix B for further information.)

Covey also stresses the importance of properly distributing advance directives. "Our position here—and it's fairly common among hospitals—is that completing the document in itself does very little for you. The more important aspect of advance directives is the dialogue and interaction that occur with the key players." The most important players are the significant members of the patient's family and his or her physician. And in the event that someone has drawn up a durable power of attorney for health care, then this attorney-in-fact would obviously be considered a key player as well.

One of the more troubling questions hospital administrators find themselves asking is whether a signed document that has never been discussed with anyone and whose appropriateness may, as a result, be questioned is better than a well-documented discussion with a physician. Given that choice, most hospitals would choose the latter. "I would say to people that it is absolutely critical when they complete their directives to discuss them with their physician and their family. They are the ones who will be involved in trying to implement them," notes Covey. To complement this approach, people would do well to place a copy of their directives in the hands of the hospital where they expect eventually to receive treatment. Since some, but by no means all, hospitals are beginning to extend this service to the community they serve, anyone interested in doing this should make inquiries at the local hospital. "But I think that's less important than having your advance directives with your physician and family members."

Medical Implications
of Advance Directives

Speaking as a hospital administrator, Covey believes that the single most important thing to be emphasized is the complexity, in medical terms, of developing advance directives. "I think all of us tend to be a little concerned about a person taking a basic living will, reading it through quickly, and signing it without having a full understanding of what it means to say, 'I want no extraordinary measures,' or, ' in the event that there is no reasonable hope of recovery,' when the reality is that the definition of 'reasonable hope,' for example, is obviously a very gray area."

Since, as we saw earlier, it is virtually impossible for people, when formulating their written directives, to anticipate the exact medical circumstances in which they will find themselves, Covey urges people to appoint a durable power of attorney for health care. "Otherwise, even with the best document in the world, if you don't have a person who has legal decision-making power, it's always a judgment call, and to some extent, you are at the whim of the physician and the hospital."

To illustrate the point, Covey compares the position of his present hospital with that of the hospital where he worked previously. Both institutions believe in cooperating to honor the advance directives of their patients. But they sharply differ in their willingness to rely on written advance directives. "In the organization here in Central Maine Medical Center, we tend to be much more conservative, in part because some judicial activity has been equivocal. Even though it has supported advance directives, it has been a little unclear about the exact circumstances in which it is appropriate to honor them." Another reason for this conservative approach, according to Covey, is the avid prolife sympathies of the current attorney general in Maine. While not opposed to the use of advance directives, this attorney general is extremely cautious about them. The result is that unless it is a straightforward case, "we are very likely to ask for another court ruling." The moral, as Covey would see it, is that in the absence of a surrogate decision maker, the patient is at the whim of the hospital where he or she is being cared for.

Federal Legislation

On 1 December 1991, new federal legislation went into effect. Known as the Patient Self-Determination Act (PSDA), this law requires institutions like hospitals and skilled nursing facilities receiving Medicare or Medicaid funding to handle advance medical directives in very specific ways. Upon admission, patients have to be informed of their rights, under state law, to refuse medical and surgical treatment. Similarly, patients have to be informed of their rights to prepare living wills and other advance directives. Upon being informed by patients that they have a living will, for example, a hospital is now obliged to indicate this in the patient's chart. But the legislation goes farther. In its concern to see that hospitals will honor advance directives, the law requires them to develop institutional policies and procedures for this purpose. And in order to ensure that these will be carried out systematically throughout the hospital, the entire professional staff of the hospital has to receive in-service training. The PSDA also requires hospitals to provide educational programs on the use of advance medical directives to all members of the public served by the particular hospital. Finally, each hospital has to prepare a statement explaining its policy for the use of advance directives and then make this available to patients on or before admission.

It is too early to say whether hospitals generally will see this legislation as an opportunity to cooperate with patients, recognizing their beliefs, values, and preferences, as they relate to medical care at the end of life. "The thing I most hope for out of this legislation" says Covey, "is that we, as hospitals, will assume a more active posture in educating people about what advance directives can do." It is important, according to Covey, for hospitals to inform their communities that the issues surrounding advance directives have importance for the community as a whole and involve complicated decisions. "They are not decisions to be made at two o'clock in the morning with two or three people huddled in a hospital room. They are decisions to be thought about well in advance."

Institutional Obstacles

Covey believes that, within the institutional setting of a hospital, patients ideally should see themselves as part of a triad that includes their own physician; the caregiver who represents the hospital itself, usually the nurse; and finally, the hospital administrators as legal arbiters of what decisions are or are not allowed within the hospital. "That becomes particularly important in a situation where a physician and a patient concur on something, and the nurse, for instance, doesn't agree." This is a frequent problem for hospitals. "We talk a lot about it at the ethics committee level, because we think that the nurse's comfort level with whatever is being done is really important. The nurse is just as likely as the disgruntled family member to be the one, sometime later, to come back to the question [of] whether things were handled appropriately—whether this person, who was allowed to die, should have been allowed to die," or, even more often, whether high-tech procedures should have been used so aggressively to prolong his or her dying.

Covey insists, however, on qualifying this observation. It does not mean that hospitals should be telling the public that in addition to completing their advance directives with physicians and family, patients also have to worry about going over them with members of the nursing staff or the administration of the institution where they will receive care. However, Covey admits that, depending on the internal policies of the hospital or the attitudes of the nursing staff, advance directives may be honored fully or may be seriously compromised.

According to the PSDA, caregivers may withdraw if they find themselves in conscientious objection to specific directives within a living will. This clause is designed to eliminate situations where the caregiver will not follow the patient's written wishes, either because of negative gut reactions or because of carefully thought out ethical positions. Everyone entering a hospital should know of this fact, but the problems surrounding caregivers' emotional reactions can be very tough. Given that, the question for a prospective patient is how to construct an advance directive in a way that will ensure its effectiveness.

Covey finds that question overwhelming. "I can't think of any way in which you can deal with that by trying to involve, for example, the caregiving nurse in your negotiating process." However, if a surrogate with authority to make decisions on behalf of the patient has also been appointed, the successful negotiation of the institution's procedures and attitudes is much more likely. The presence of a person who can confirm that the actual clinical situation is indeed similar to the situation anticipated by the patient when he or she developed an advance directive provides a critical level of assurance for the hospital.

Disagreement between doctors and nurses within the hospital occurs frequently. It often comes to light in the proceedings of an ethics committee. In such instances, the case has been presented along with an ethical analysis and the treatment decision to which this has led. "Then somebody will say, 'Tell me about the other caretakers. Has any disagreement been expressed?'" In many cases, the nurses seriously disagree with the decision.

Covey tends to attribute such disagreements between doctors and nurses to their need for substantially more education in this area. "I don't think the medical profession is anywhere nearly as well educated as it needs to be. What you find is that the nurses—and the physicians, for that matter—haven't thought the issues through in a reasonable way from an ethical perspective."

Another institutional obstacle to thoughtful decision making is concern over legal liability. "From the hospital's point of view and the physician's point of view," says Covey, "much of the turmoil around these issues, much of the struggling that we go through on these issues is driven by a risk-management posture." The premise from which this posture has been derived is that the institution is in a less risky legal position if it errs on the side of maintaining life. Generally speaking, most people would agree with the premise, particularly where the clinical circumstances are unclear. Living will statutes have attempted to address this issue by including clauses that provide institutional and professional individual immunity to those who, in good faith, provide or withhold medical treatment according to the terms of individual advance directives. The PSDA contains similar clauses. Despite that, hospitals and physicians alike are wary about providing or withholding treatment. "Obviously, there is legal exposure in either direction."

According to Covey, another force influencing the ethos of

modern hospitals stems from medical technology. "We have this incredible technology, and there's a very seductive quality about it. You get physicians and other care providers who fall in love with what the technology is able to do and, because of that, probably tend to be too quick to use or to overuse it." He is, of course, alluding to the so-called technological imperative discussed earlier. In the hospital setting this finds expression in the tendency of medical staff to do all they have been trained to do without attempting to balance the burdens and benefits to the patient.[3] Together with the practice of "defensive medicine" as a way of avoiding liability, the technological imperative is, according to Covey, a key force within the hospital setting that everyone needs to recognize when preparing their advance medical directives.

Content of Advance Directives

As we saw earlier, many physicians prefer to see living wills and other advance directives couched in statements of personal values rather than in statements of clinical specifics. Speaking from the perspective of the hospital, Covey would like to see advance directives contain both. Since it is impossible to develop an exhaustive list of clinical specifics, the statement of values can be a most important part of any living will. Statements of value, however, are not without their own drawbacks. "I see physicians dealing in specifics, dealing in specific clinical issues, and those statements of values can be pretty broadly interpreted by physicians, depending upon their own persuasions and their own sense of what a reasonable quality of life is. That's the concern I have about limiting it to the values statement."

Hospitals, once they recognize some of the difficulties involved in complying with the terms of individual advance directives, can take the initiative to assist the process. "One of the things we have started to do, something I think hospitals are going to have to do a lot more of, is in the area of policy and protocol development." Currently, Covey's hospital is developing what he describes as a limited therapy policy, which is a broader version of a do-not-resuscitate policy. It is not restricted to cardiopulmonary resuscitation and includes limitations to a range of life-sustaining treatments. Covey considers hospital policy development a critical way to complement patients' efforts to determine the boundaries of treatment. In the absence of institutional policies and protocols, hospitals are rudderless and their patients suffer accordingly. The more he has seen hospitals develop their protocols and establish in advance a process for making decisions, says Covey, the better it has been for both the institutions themselves and the people they serve.

Special Questions in the Nursing Home

While much of what is contained in this section is written in relation to the hospital setting, it also applies for the most part to the nursing home setting. Nevertheless, there are one or two points that are of great relevance to the nursing home. In particular, there is the critical need for surrogate decision makers. Since greater longevity increasingly occasions loss of capacity to make medical decisions, a major consideration in the preparation of advance directives should be the appointment of a relative or friend with legal authority to make these decisions on your behalf in the event that you are unable to make them for yourself.

Not only is it important to select your surrogate carefully, it is important that this person fully understands what your medical choices might be, along with the values and beliefs that prompt them. Indeed, there is every reason to think that a clear communication of your values and beliefs is indispensable since your surrogate may have to make decisions under clinical circumstances that were not specifically anticipated by you.

In relation to the nursing home, it is important to understand the actual role of the physician. There is ample anecdotal evidence which suggests that physicians play by different rules in the nursing home setting, depending upon their interest in treating older people and the extent to which they are inclined to use medical technology. Complicating this is the ambivalence many physicians feel about discussing treatment decisions at the end of life with nursing home residents. They do not want to be involved, preferring to leave those discussions to the nursing home staff. At the same time, physicians can resent the fact that other professionals are discussing very important issues with their patients, fearing the outcome of discussions in which they have had little or no part. Because of this it is very important, before entering a nursing home, to come to some clear understandings with your physician about his or her role in your treatment at the end of life.

One of the obvious advantages that nursing homes enjoy over hospitals is, generally speaking, the absence of any urgency to make decisions immediately. The nature of chronic illness and long-term care is such that it affords the time to make thoughtful decisions. Provided physicians and nursing home staff are willing, residents can weigh the benefits over the burdens of continuing treatments at the end of life. A resident, stable population makes this possible in ways clearly not available in other institutional settings, such as a hospital, for example. But here there are dangers. Professional staff in a nursing home is not nearly as diversified as that in a hospital, and there is nothing like the professional monitoring of staff in nursing homes commonly found in hospitals. As a result, a distinctly homogeneous set of attitudes is likely to exert a much more direct influence on residents in discussions about treatment at the end of life. Nursing home staff may rely on their purely personal sense of what is ethically appropriate, rather than measure objectively the ethical implications of specific treatments and their alternatives. In particular, the decision to withdraw or withhold artificial nutrition and hydration is expected to become the focus of increasing controversy in the years ahead.

IN THE INTENSIVE CARE UNIT

Mrs. G. is a seventy-two-year-old woman with severe lung disease related to a history of heavy smoking. During a hospitalization for an episode of pneumonia, she stopped breathing. She was then placed on a ventilator in hopes of supporting her lung function until the antibiotics could take effect against the pneumonia. After three weeks she is still in the intensive care unit (ICU) and has developed pressure sores on her buttocks, and a bladder infection from a bladder catheter. Usually confused and disoriented, she is receiving regular doses of antipsychotic tranquilizers to keep her from pulling out her tubes—she has two intravenous lines, a nasogastric feeding tube, a bladder catheter, and the ventilator tube. Often the nurses are forced to restrain her hands to keep her from removing these tubes and lines. She is too weak and confused to be weaned from the ventilator. The doctors are hopeful that once the bladder infection is controlled, she'll become strong enough to breathe on her own. Her husband and adult sons have never talked to her about her wishes for care under these types of circumstances, but they are convinced that she is suffering and miserable. No one has seen any improvement in her condition since she came to the ICU. If anything, she seems to be getting worse.

The worse a patient becomes, the greater the temptation is to use all that an intensive care unit has to offer. In cases like Mrs. G., that course of action appears increasingly questionable. "The intensive care unit is the one place where medicine, technology, society, and ethics confront each other on a minute-to-minute basis."[4] Since it is such a critical crossroads, the ICU presents particular challenges to the use of living wills and health proxies. Some familiarity with its purpose and experience will help in making these advance directives clearer and more specific.

The Experience of an Intensive Care Unit

Patients find themselves in an intensive care unit when their doctors feel that they need "constant attention and care."[5] Fitted with an array of very sophisticated instruments and staffed by highly trained nurses and technicians, the ICU provides precise and prompt care to patients in critical condition.

The first experience of an ICU can be alarming for patients and their families. June Bingham, author of *You and the ICU*,[6] first encountered the intensive care unit when her critically ill husband was a patient at the Columbia-Presbyterian Medical Center in New York. It was not a pleasant experience: "I couldn't find his face. There was nothing but blue tubes. I had to look and look and look for him."[7] Her reaction combined a sense of horror at the mechanical domination of the patient and gratitude because, in her husband's case, a respirator had saved his life. "I think one bit of counsel to families of patients is that you will almost never have a pure emotion; they're all mixed. You're on a roller coaster of hope and despair."

This experience prompted Bingham to design a program of assistance for families of patients in intensive care units so that they could handle the harrowing emotional difficulties presented by an ICU. The first and most obvious of these might be the first impression. There is glass everywhere and little privacy. A deliberate design, it permits a small number of highly trained caregivers to provide constant and immediate care to a larger number of very sick patients.

A second source of dismay can be the forest of tubes attached to the patient. Some of these, like the plastic IV (intravenous) tubes, bring medication or nourishment into the patient's bloodstream. Another, a nasogastric tube inserted through the nose, conveys liquid food directly into the patient's stomach. Yet another plastic tube, called a catheter, drains urine from the patient.

Perhaps the most noticeable machine is the respirator, because it is so noisy. Designed to pump oxygen into the bloodstream, the respirator is extremely sensitive and needs to be adjusted frequently. If, for example, the patient's breathing pattern deviates from that of the respirator, an alarm will sound to alert the monitoring technician to make any necessary adjustments.

Patients are under constant monitoring. Over each patient looms a camera connected to a video terminal at the nurses' station. A bedside monitor transfers an instant record of the patient's heartbeat to the nurses' terminal. Any significant change in rhythm will automatically trigger an alarm and alert the staff. In the event of cardiac arrest, a defibrillating machine and an external pacemaker are there for immediate use.

According to C. David Finley, M.D., the director of intensive care at St. Lukes–Roosevelt Medical Center in New York, understanding how an intensive care unit functions and how it affects the ICU staff is very important for anyone trying to compose a realistic advance medical directive. "Intensive care is extremely technologically advanced and provided in a very dehumanized, depersonalized environment."[8] The array of digital displays and intense monitoring of patients dominate the intensive care unit. This is necessary because the purpose of the unit is to deal with acute illnesses that demand very complicated care. Medical and nursing staff working in this environment typically focus on the patients and their symptoms to the exclusion of practically everything else, including the patients' family members. This combination of clinical single-mindedness and technological sophistication can make an ICU alienating and uninviting for a visiting member of the patient's family. "Often," says Finley, "it's no one's specific duty to introduce the family to the unit and to the procedures that might be carried out there."

The situation is difficult in another sense. Family members have a very clear need to be informed about the medical condition of the patient. In addition, they probably need a great deal of reassurance if they are going to participate effectively at critical decision-making points. At the same time, medical and nursing staff are under constant pressure as they work to provide medical care for the patient. And if that meticulously planned care finds itself in competition with family needs for the attention of the ICU staff, family needs will invariably lose. If one family member is selected, through whom all communication with the staff will go, this conflict is less likely to arise.

If the environment of the intensive care unit is disturbing for the family, it is even more so for patients. In this completely unfamiliar setting, they are, understandably, afraid of both their illness and the treatment it requires. As they, quite naturally, think about their chances of recovery, they can become very anxious. At no time do they need the support of their family more, but the very nature of the ICU is such that it seriously restricts contact between patient and family. At a time when patients most need the support, they find themselves most alone. "I believe strongly that the role of the family in an illness that requires treatment in an intensive care unit is as important as the role of nurses and doctors," says Finley, pointing out that in those cases where patients have a strong support system, such as a family working closely together, better medical outcomes are more likely.

The nature of intensive care units takes virtually all control away from patients. Often they do not eat of their own accord, nor do they clean themselves. They have no physical activity except at the discretion of the nursing staff or on a physician's order. Consequently, there is a pervasive sense of dependency on others. At the same time, most patients feel an acute need—ironically, more pronounced in the ICU—to exercise greater personal control. "And so, one of the things that you see in an intensive care unit is a strong tendency to act things out. Families need to express their concerns. Patients need to exercise control over an environment that takes all control from them." It is not surprising, says Finley, that in such a situation there is always something to cause conflict.

Because care has to be provided literally twenty-four hours a day, activity in an intensive care unit is constant. The lights are always on, people talk constantly, and members of the staff work in continuous shifts around the clock. The result is an unrelenting onslaught on the human system accustomed to diurnal rhythms of waking and sleeping, activity and rest, the light of day and the darkness of night. One of the greatest problems for the patients in this setting can be sensory deprivation side by side with sensory overload. They are removed from family and a familiar environment and now find themselves in a setting so alien that there is no real expectation of adjusting in any reasonable sense. At the same time, they are subjected to continuous stimulation from light, noise, and activity. Caught in such a siege of the senses, patients, not surprisingly, become disoriented, angry, and hostile. "They tend to act out just in response to the environment, or they will withdraw totally, become depressed and more and more introverted." Whatever the reaction, it is clear that the physical demands of an intensive care unit can take a tremendous toll on individual patients.

The Staff of an Intensive Care Unit

One of the biggest practical problems for both patient and family is understanding which people are in charge of nursing practice and physician practice in an intensive care unit so as not to confuse them with people responsible for other areas of activity within a unit. One of the frustrations common to family members is taking what rightly is a problem to the wrong person. When that happens, they can feel inadequate or sometimes even guilty for failing to pursue the problem through to an acceptable resolution. This also raises fears that the system is inefficient or, worse, simply does not work. "By and large, that's not really true," says Finley. "You

just need to know how to work the system." With one member
appointed to serve as the liaison with key staff members in a
systematic and predictable way, families can overcome much confusion. "Under those circumstances, you will find the more organized and directed you are, the more organized and responsive the
system is to you. When families do not communicate well, or
there is no leadership on their side, things on our side break down
as well."

Although there is no standard form, the staffing of an intensive
care unit is usually based on two general factors: (1) the severity
of the patients' medical condition and (2) the number of patients.
Typically, one nurse is assigned to two patients. If the patients are
not terribly ill, their condition is reasonably stable, and they do
not require a lot of detailed treatment, one nurse can be expected
to care for three patients. But often the patients are so ill that each
needs one nurse dedicated to his or her individual care.

Most ICUs will be managed so as to provide a staff nurse who
is at the patient's bedside giving care. In addition, there is a clinical
nurse specialist who monitors the quality of the care that is actually being given. Finally, there is a clinical coordinator who over-
sees policy and procedures, as well as disciplinary and management issues relating to the way the unit is run. All of these people
are on site in the unit, and they are responsible, in shifts, for
running its nursing activities twenty-four hours a day, seven days
a week.

There is also a medical team. The leader of this group will often
be the patient's own physician. If the patient does not have a
private doctor, the attending physician in the unit itself will act in
that capacity. The medical team also includes a senior medical
resident, two or three second-year medical residents, and a number of physicians completing their internships.

Since the intensive care unit functions through team management, the medical outcomes are best when all members of the unit
function well as a team. Clinical rounds, a process that involves
visiting the patients and reviewing their diagnosis and prognosis,
is ideally done as a team. This approach ensures that the nursing
management goals and the medical management goals, which
often are different, can be carefully discussed and coordinated.

In an ICU the differences between these two sets of goals can be pronounced. For example, a patient who has been on a ventilator is about to be taken off. Before doing so, the medical team typically checks the patient's blood gases to ensure a stable condition and a good response on the machine. But the nursing team may be aware of something else that is equally important. Maintaining excellent blood gas levels requires suctioning every twenty minutes. As a result, the patient has not slept in the previous forty-eight hours and is, understandably, physically exhausted. "If the two teams shared their respective information, they might be on more common ground in making major medical management decisions," says Finley. Physicians do not always see the extent of care and management provided by the nursing team in the case of a particular patient. In turn, nurses are not always entirely sensitive to physicians' degree of involvement in managing the patient's care. The reality is that the care of the patient in the ICU is continuous, but continuous along separate tracks for the physicians and the nurses. "They need to work harder to explore their common interests and some of their differences to effect a plan that will maximize benefits for the patient."

Those who work in intensive care units are generally people who like to take charge and make decisions, enjoying the unexpectedness and spontaneity so typical of a setting where change is the norm. On the hospital floor or in a clinic, where patients are awake, alert, and capable, there may be more opportunities for close, caring, and supportive relationships between patient and caregivers. In an extremely automated clinical setting like an ICU, the tendency not to relate to people is pronounced. "It's easier sometimes to sedate a patient than it is to reassure him; it's easier to look at the blood gas than to use your clinical judgment," says Finley. "There's a tendency to rely on objective documentation because, in part, that's what we do. And that may be unfortunate."

During rounds in an intensive care unit, the main focus is on tests and on each patient's electrolytes, diagnosis, and treatment. Rarely is there any discussion of who the patients are or how they feel about their situation. Little attention is paid to the patients' understanding of their disease, and probably less to their sense of what the clinical outcomes might be. No formal procedures are in place for informing members of the family so that they can support the patient's care. Often those working in the intensive care setting cannot actually interact with the patient on a personal level, but they can always work with the family. If healing is to be accompanied by caring, nurses and physicians must understand that some of their services are not for the patient at all but for the family. But the truth is that in ICUs much remains to be done by all of the staff to include the family in the process of providing care to the patient.

The Role of the Family

Whether family members are included by the staff may depend largely on the behavior of family members themselves. When doctors and nurses cannot enlist a patient's consent and active participation, they need the family to play a very responsible role. But some family members do not want to assume this responsibility, preferring instead a passive role. "I think that the patient who can no longer represent himself has a bond and trust with his family to represent him in the way he would have represented himself, were he able to," says Finley. Such representation is critical but not always offered. All too often, patients who have become dependent on others to convey their personal preferences and values are simply let down by their family.

Another reason for this need is the nature of the institution. A hospital, for example, will continue to do what it views as its job. It will order the tests, provide the treatments, and continue rendering care—all as part of its function. "The fact that these things are inappropriate or unwanted from the patient's point of view can only be known by the family," says Finley. "I think they have a responsibility to come forward and be clear, not only about what they know, but how they know it." In the face of modern medical practice, two of the essential rational justifications for any decision to treat or not is our knowledge of the patient's preferences and our obligation to protect the patient. "If you know that a person would not want to be connected to a respirator and given artificial feeding, you have a responsibility to see to it that they are stopped. Otherwise, you have lost the integrity of that person forever."

Using the Living Will Wisely

The patient's living will, if it is introduced in a timely manner, can determine the subsequent course of events. Unfortunately, it is not unusual to see a family using the living will at the very last moment as though it were a trump card. Sometimes this behavior is dictated by a fear that the living will actually puts the patient at risk of not receiving the kind of care his or her condition requires. Similarly, family members sometimes fear that, by presenting a living will, they may appear to be doubting the staff's interest in the patient's well-being. So strong is their fear of alienating doctors and nurses, that family members tend to overlook the fact that as long as a living will remains unknown, its contents can play no part in making critical medical decisions. "I think the biggest tragedy is when, after weeks and weeks of treatment, we discover that the patient has a living will [when] knowing that at the outset would have changed dramatically the patient's care and outcome."

It is, therefore, in everybody's interest to present the living will upon admission. Contrary to what one might think, it is not necessarily being pessimistic about one's medical condition to say that, in the event of a life-threatening problem, this is how one would choose to be treated. Nor is it rational to think that saying what approach one prefers in case of a life-threatening condition could ever cause the condition to happen. What does happen is that patients take account of the possibility of the unexpected. By declaring in advance to family and doctors the preferences for medical treatment and the values that dictate those preferences, patients can ensure that *these* values and preferences do in fact inform any medical decisions that are made on their behalf. The patient, says Finley, "is the only person who benefits from that because he is the only person who will suffer the consequences if they cannot be determined or they are delayed in their presentation."

IN A HOSPICE

For many persons faced with the last stages of a terminal illness, hospice care offers the best setting in which to have their wishes for end-of-life treatment honored. Over the past twenty years, hospices have been established all across the United States with the expressed mission of providing comfortable, nurturing, non-intrusive treatment to incurably ill people. And more and more patients are choosing a hospice—as opposed to the hospital ward or intensive care unit—as the place to spend their final days. In England, where the modern hospice movement began, most hospices are freestanding institutions, where round-the-clock professional care is provided. The situation is much different in the United States, where home-care hospice programs have spread rapidly to meet the needs of the vast number of patients who wish to die at home. In these programs, professional palliative care and support services are brought directly to the client on a routine basis. In the United States, these are much more common than hospices that offer inpatient care.

At first glance, hospice philosophies and those of most advance directives designed to limit treatment appear to overlap almost exactly. "When you choose hospice care," explains Jeanne Dennis, M.S.W., the hospice administrator for New York City's Visiting Nurse Service, "you're making a statement right there about the type of treatment you want. You're saying, in effect, that you are only seeking basic palliative care—that you don't wish to be resuscitated or ventilated or kept alive by other artificial means."[9] The standard consent forms that each patient must sign state clearly that no "artificial or heroic means" will be used and no "aggressive treatment" will be administered to patients while they are under the care of the hospice program. Although these forms and the underlying criteria and guidelines for care may vary from hospice to hospice, the basic message is always the same: The purpose of hospice is to provide relief from the distressing symptoms of terminal illness, to reduce pain and make the patient as comfortable as possible, and to offer spiritual and emotional support—*not* to sustain life by artificial means. Those who choose hospice care have accepted the inevitability and the nearness of death; they seek assistance in facing their approaching illness and death in as comfortable and pain-free an environment as possible.

It is, in fact, precisely the clarity and precision of the hospice mission that limit it as an option for many people considering their wishes for end-of-life treatment *before* a terminal illness or

critical injury occurs. While each hospice may have its own separate criteria for admission, all are limited by the time restrictions
of federal hospice Medicare benefits to the care of patients with
(1) no expected cure and (2) a prognosis of less than six months.
This represents a reasonable description of people with certain
types of terminal illnesses, such as leukemia and other cancers,
which the hospice system was originally designed to manage.
Unfortunately, many other illnesses are automatically excluded,
especially those in which a deteriorating condition in the terminal
stage of the disease is more prolonged or unpredictable. And, of
course, victims of sudden, incapacitating injury are left out altogether, since trauma patients, however near to death they may be
or dependent for their survival on life-sustaining treatment, are
not technically terminally ill by any generally accepted medical
standards or existing laws.

Despite these limitations, hospice care offers much to those
patients whose illnesses and prognoses fit the criteria for admission. For these people, perhaps the most important factor in
choosing a hospice program, as well as in any other discussions
around advance planning, is making sure that the treatment
guidelines and restrictions really do meet their wishes and needs.

According to Jeanne Dennis, most problems and complications—at least for cancer patients—arise around the use of
artificial hydration and nutrition. "There's always the case," explains Dennis of a typical situation, "of the patient suffering from
a large tumor in his or her belly. The patient is totally obstructed,
and no matter what you try, they just can't swallow a thing or keep
anything down. In such a case, the decision not to use artificial
feeding or hydration means that the patient is going to die within
a couple of weeks—no question about it. But," she continues, "if
to use [artificial] feeding and hydration might mean spending a
couple of extra months in reasonable comfort, with family,
friends, and the things one enjoys, most hospice workers would
agree that you should at least raise these treatments as an option,
even within a hospice setting."

Under the guidelines of some hospices, however, such considerations would be ruled out in advance because they would
violate the specific terms of the patient's consent to treatment.
"Each hospice program has its own criteria for admission and

care," warns Dennis, "and some of them are quite rigid. With regard to hydration or nutrition, for example, the policy of some programs might be, 'If you need that, you can have it; but you can't get it from us.' " For this reason, patients or future patients considering hospice care need to be well educated about the admission policies and guidelines for treatment of the particular hospice program they are considering, and equally clear and articulate about their own wishes *before* entrusting themselves to its care.

Another recent complication in hospice care and planning has been the dramatic impact of the AIDS epidemic. As the demand for long-term, palliative care for persons in the terminal stage of AIDS has increased, many hospice programs have opened their doors to people with AIDS, even though the patients often do not meet the formal requirements for admission, due to the unpredictable nature of the illness. And since AIDS research and treatment are changing so rapidly, many AIDS patients are being treated with experimental drugs, even as they seek palliative care in the final stages of their illness. Because of this situation, hospices that serve clients with AIDS are sometimes willing to allow the use of aggressive or experimental treatments in cases where such treatments offer the possibility of reversing, not simply managing, the life-threatening symptoms of the disease.

All these changes make it even more important that a person considering hospice care have ongoing, advance discussions with family and professional caregivers about end-of-life care *before* making actual arrangements for treatment. As with terminal care in a hospital, this process should include not only a living will but also identification of another person (or persons) to serve as a proxy decision maker in the event that one is incapacitated by the progression of illness. Since much hospice care is home care, hospice consent forms routinely stipulate that another person outside the hospice team must identify himself or herself as a primary caretaker for the patient. This person agrees not only to manage and provide the ongoing care of the patient, especially during those times when the professional staff is unavailable, but, according to Dennis, "also consents to being available to help with managing business for and making decisions on behalf of the patient if the patient becomes incompetent." Recent health-care-proxy and other surrogate-decision-making legislation has complicated the matter by providing specific, and sometimes restrictive, guidelines for substituted judgment and terminal care decision making. Therefore, if you are in a hospice program, it is crucial that the person you choose as your primary caretaker be fully familiar with such state health-care-proxy laws.

As patients have become increasingly knowledgeable about their conditions and the various options available for treatment, the old extremes—of "life at all costs" versus "absolutely no artificial treatment"—have become less and less adequate for many people. "We're seeing more and more patients we are admitting who have a living will along with their hospice consent form," reports Dennis. "And we're also getting a lot more patients who have already appointed proxies to make decisions on their behalf." Patients today are finding that even entrusting their final care to the hospice system—where nonintrusive, palliative care is the unapologetic goal—is often not enough. Those who wish to direct the treatment they will receive at the end of life—even if they are totally incapacitated by illness or trauma—must still spell out their wishes clearly, convincingly, and in advance. In addition, they must designate and prepare another person to speak on their behalf.

NOTES

1. Molly Cooke, interview with authors, February 1991. All subsequent quotations from Dr. Cooke cited in this chapter are from this interview.
2. Laird Covey, interview with authors, March 1991. All subsequent quotations from Mr. Covey cited in this chapter are from this interview.
3. See V. R. Fuchs, *Who Shall Live? Health, Economics and Social Choice* (New York: Basic Books, 1974).
4. Thomas A. Raffin, Joel N. Shurkin, and Wharton Sinkler III, *Intensive Care: Facing the Critical Choices* (New York: Freeman, 1989), 7.
5. Ibid, 3.
6. June Bingham et al., *You and the ICU* (New York: Presbyterian Hospital, 1990), 1.
7. June Bingham, interview with authors, January 1991. All subsequent quotations from Ms. Bingham cited in this chapter are from this interview.
8. C. David Finley, interview with authors, January 1991. All subsequent quotations from Dr. Finley cited in this chapter are from this interview.
9. Jeanne Dennis, interview with authors, October 1991. All subsequent quotations from Ms. Dennis are from this interview.

SIX

Easing Pain and Symptoms

It is fear that I stand most in fear of;
in sharpness it exceeds every other feeling.

MONTAIGNE
Essays

Not long ago, Mr. T., a seventy-two-year-old man with advanced prostate cancer was admitted to the hospital with dehydration and fever. In the past few months, he and his family had discussed his illness and the treatments he would want as the disease progressed. Although he had not drawn up a living will, it was clear that he wanted no aggressive efforts to keep him alive once he was in severe pain and no longer alert.

When he was admitted to the hospital, Mr. T. was rather confused; he had a urinary tract infection and signs of early kidney failure, and he was under sedation. Intravenous fluids and antibiotics were administered, and he became more alert. Then, however, he began to complain of pain radiating in both legs. The pain increased, and Mr. T. was given escalating doses of a strong narcotic drug. The increasing doses and the progressive kidney failure made him foggy and out of touch with those around him.

To improve his awareness, the drug dosage was lowered, but he immediately felt severe pain. At the request of the family, the pain medication was increased, while antibiotics, fluids, and other treatment of his symptoms continued. His condition became more stable for awhile.

75

Three weeks later, Mr. T. became much sicker. His kidneys nearly ceased working, and there was evidence of fluid in his lungs. Realizing that he was near death, his family asked whether a change in the pain therapy could temporarily make him more lucid, so that they could say goodbye. The doctor thought that this might be possible, since the narcotic drugs being used were the main reason he was not alert. But the doctor also said that, in his clinical judgment, any aggressive efforts to awaken Mr. T. were inappropriate, given the advanced state of his disease. The family and physician agreed to intensive efforts to reverse the patient's medical problems, initially without a change in pain therapy. If these efforts should stabilize his condition again, the physician would try alternative pain therapies, which might leave him more alert and perhaps even enable him to spend a little more time at home. None of the medical measures were successful, however, and Mr. T.'s kidneys failed entirely. Four days later, he died in a peaceful coma.

PROBLEMS IN PAIN CONTROL

The consideration of pain and its control is such a vital part of planning for terminal care that a living will which leaves out instructions for the management of pain is seriously incomplete. Adequate directives for pain management are not easy, however. They require self-understanding and information about an issue that is poorly understood by both the medical profession itself and lay persons. Complicating this is the fact that in practice the managing of pain raises a number of ethical and legal dilemmas for both the patient and the doctor, in particular the question of assisted suicide. Also making the issue complex is the fact that individuals vary enormously in their ability and their willingness to tolerate pain. As a result, apart from the medical issues, the need for pain control will be as varied as the individuals for whom it is being provided.

Fear of pain takes at least two forms: fear of the pain itself and fear of the inability to control pain. Of the two, the second is the greater fear. While many of us would accept that physical pain may be inevitable at some point in the course of a fatal illness, most of us do not accept that an inability to control pain is inevitable. Anyone who asks, "Doctor, can't you do something for this pain?" is assuming that something can be done to make the pain go away.

While this may be true in some absolute sense, the everyday reality in many hospitals is that pain is poorly managed. Patients suffer extensive and intense pain far more widely than is necessary. While undertreatment is usually the cause, the full explanation is more complicated. For one thing, many doctors and nurses lack the technical training to treat pain in a sophisticated and effective manner. They are not good at assessing and then treating pain in their patients. But more importantly, their fears of the side effects of the drugs used to relieve pain are, by any acceptable measure of prudence, quite unreasonable. The fact is that drugs are available and techniques have been developed to control pain successfully at levels that are bearable for most patients, and without life-threatening or addictive side-effects.

How seriously ought the fear of addiction be taken? Russell K. Portenoy, the director of pain research at Memorial Sloan-Kettering Hospital in New York, says that this fear is vastly overblown. "There's a huge clinical experience that suggests that addiction—true addiction—is a rare phenomenon when patients are treated with opioid drugs for painful medical diseases like cancer."[1]

The problem, it seems, is one of definition. Portenoy believes that many patients and their families, as well as clinicians, confuse physical dependence on a drug with actual addiction. But clinically, they are distinct. It is true that patients being treated for pain, for a long enough period of time, with an opioid drug can become physically dependent on it. But that dependence is characteristic of the pharmacology of the drug itself and becomes visible only as a withdrawal symptom when the drug is withdrawn suddenly. Properly weaned from a drug therapy, the patient will not normally manifest withdrawal. In contrast, according to the World Health Organization, the American Medical Association, and numerous other professional organizations, addiction is a *psychological dependence* expressing itself through drug craving. The craving is so intense that it produces aberrant behaviors, such as hoarding drugs, using them more frequently or in greater amounts than prescribed, or obtaining them from more than one source. A patient who is addicted might, for example, be found making frequent visits to the hospital emergency room or scheming so that unwitting medical staff will provide higher doses of drugs.

From this it is clear that addictive behavior occurs because the patient has become psychologically dependent on the use of drugs. But numerous studies of cancer patients receiving drug therapies for pain, for example, have demonstrated that psychological dependence is extremely rare. This is particularly true in the case of patients who, before their illness, have no history of addictive behavior. "This reality," says Portenoy, "for some reason, has not filtered down to the patient, the patient's family, and very often the patient's primary physician, many of whom are worried that the use of these drugs is going to cause the patient to become addicted."

Those who specialize in pain research believe that the fear of addiction makes good pain management very difficult. This unnecessary anxiety can become one more burden for a patient and family, already physically and emotionally overwhelmed, to bear in the course of an illness. As a result, this anxiety can also interfere seriously with patients' willingness to comply faithfully with their therapy.

In a particularly ironic way, this fear of addiction can do even more harm. Recently, researchers have described a problem called *pseudo-addiction*. Similar to real addiction, this is a pattern of behavior caused by the inadequate management of a patient's pain. According to Portenoy, "There are patients who will make multiple visits to emergency rooms, who will go doctor-shopping, who will make frequent telephone calls to their physician, demonstrating a kind of aggressive, drug-seeking behavior which can be interpreted as a dangerous sign of addiction." In reality, this behavior is being caused by the fear of pain itself, in turn brought about by poor management of their pain on the part of those who are more worried about addiction than the patients' welfare. Once the pain is well managed, these pseudo-addictive patterns of behavior disappear.

At the same time, accurate measurement of levels of pain being experienced by patients has remained elusive. Both caregivers and patients often find it difficult to assess pain, mainly because it is hard to describe what is essentially a subjective experience. In the absence of measurable criteria, the tendency for medical and nursing staff is to measure a patient's pain by analogy, that is, in terms of their own experience of pain. This may be another reason why treatment for pain has been less than adequate. Complicating this is the experience of many patients that when they describe their symptoms too graphically, the doctors and nurses often react skeptically. As a result, patients are reluctant even to mention their symptoms of pain for fear of appearing to be complainers. Nobody likes a complainer, and in their vulnerable situation, patients, perhaps more than anyone else, feel the need to be liked. They may also worry that if they complain, they will receive poor care. Another factor here is the tendency of patients, when talking to doctors and nurses, to focus on their disease rather than their symptoms, including pain. Finally, even if an accurate measure of pain were obtainable, the fact that overwork prevents hospital staff from properly evaluating the needs of their patients, coupled with a shortage of nurses trained to administer pain medication, means that patients continue to experience pain unnecessarily.

WHAT PATIENTS AND FAMILIES CAN DO

As long as this state of affairs persists, education about pain and its treatment is as high a priority as any possible planning for terminal care. Everyone writing a living will should know that pain is very often the main threat to an acceptable quality of life. Everyone should also know that it is possible to manage pain satisfactorily, if not completely, when available therapies are used with skill. While the risk of suffering side-effects exists, the risk is relatively low, and side-effects that do occur can usually be managed. Patients should also know the importance of informing their doctors of the pain they feel and their need to know whether pain will be managed well as their disease progresses.

Russell Portenoy points out that unrelieved symptoms contribute to a patient's overall suffering and that suffering, in turn, contributes to the decisions that are made at the end of life by both patient and physician. "I think that the degree to which a patient suffers influences tremendously the clinical decision making at that phase of the disease." He explains that a patient who is comfortable represents a different set of challenges to those presented by a patient who is very uncomfortable. "Patients who are comfortable and see that there is some high quality of life left may be willing to be resuscitated in an acute situation where there's the possibility of a reversal, whereas patients who are suffering very much may be opposed to that." Similarly, there is strong evidence indicating that physicians who consider their patients to have been relatively comfortable and functioning well, despite the advanced stage of their disease, will order invasive procedures, including resuscitation, to deal with temporary critical situations if they feel they can restabilize the patient's condition. By the same token, physicians will probably not treat terminally ill patients who, prior to an intervening complication have been in extreme pain simply because the patients aren't likely to experience any benefit. If the prevailing quality of life of the patient is poor, the risks of aggressive treatment are greater than any benefit derived from it. "So I see the degree of suffering that the patient is expressing at this phase of their disease as having tremendous repercussions on all of the critical decisions made by the health-care provider, and also on the way patients view their own condition and their own desire to be treated."

Clear communication, particularly on the part of the patient, is therefore critical. Patients can and should take the lead in communicating. Most doctors and nurses would welcome their doing so, because the caregivers have a genuine interest in finding out what will best relieve suffering for an individual patient. First, patients must find a way to convey accurately the extent of their pain. Whatever form that description takes, the more concrete the better. Russell Portenoy suggests that they say, "I have this symptom which is generally moderate or generally severe in intensity and which is preventing me from doing specific things, things that I really want to do now." By conveying a sense of the intensity of the pain and its level of interference with specific activities, the patient probably provides the doctors and nurses with the information most useful for their treatment decisions. To say that the pain is excruciating is one thing. To say that it is so bad that "it is preventing me from sleeping/walking/sitting upright, and so on" is far more useful when clinical decisions about treatment have to be made.

The more patients and their families know about the options for treating pain, the more effective their requests can be. Besides narcotic and anti-inflammatory drugs, there are nonpharmacological means such as radiotherapy, neurosurgery, electrical stimulation, and psychological approaches.

It is also important to know how pain medication can be administered. The most common way by far is to swallow drugs orally. Perhaps one of the most important things for patients to know is that they can control their own pain medication. After careful consultation, patients can arrange through an order from their physician to receive the necessary medication as it is needed. This is known as "pain relief as needed" (PRN). It is not without drawbacks, however. According to Ronald Melzack,[2] a leading pain researcher at the Pain Rehabilitaion Research Unit of the Department of Psychiatry, McGill University, Montreal, the pain prescription, "as needed," means that the drug is provided *after* the patient has begun to experience pain again. He also points out that the PRN approach frequently leads to confrontation between patients and the caregiver, whose expectation is that the pain medication will last four to six hours. "The patient, whose pain has returned earlier than expected, is in agony and pleads to have the next injection. The health-care worker, fearful of causing addiction, refuses to comply." Melzack adds that when the pain is finally treated, it may be so severe that a larger dose has to be given, increasing the probability of side effects such as mental clouding and nausea. He concludes that in the case of terminal patients, any fear of addiction is meaningless and delays in providing relief are cruel.

Even more direct control is now possible because of technological developments. By means of an infusion pump programmed by a microcomputer, the patient can press a button and receive a predetermined amount of medication for pain control. It might be thought that with such direct and easy control, patients would be inclined to administer their drugs more than is necessary. But studies have shown not only that patients did not overuse their pain-killing drugs, but that they reduced their use of pain medication as the level of pain declined.

PAIN RELIEF AND EUTHANASIA

In addition to these clinical questions, the treatment of pain raises ethical questions of particular concern to those preparing a living will or appointing a health-care proxy. The most obvious has to do with the potential relationship of pain medication and euthanasia. At certain levels, medication required to control pain, particularly when patients are close to death, can depress breathing and as a result quicken the onset of death. Does this mean that by administering pain relief under such circumstances and with these results the patient or the caregiver is engaged in euthanasia?

Pain-management specialists view suicide and euthanasia on the one hand, and pain management on the other, as quite different. In support of their view, they can advance statistical data showing that suicide among cancer patients, for example, is very rare. Within the same population, even thoughts of suicide and attempts are extremely rare. Most patients who think about suicide do so because of unrelieved symptoms. In other words, when patients can enjoy a liberal use of narcotics to relieve pain, they are comfortable. When patients are comfortable, they tend to cope better; and when patients feel that they can cope, they are not inclined to commit suicide.

The more difficult issue is the concern that aggressive pain management, particularly at the end stage of a disease, is the equivalent of euthanasia. Since pain therapies can and do accelerate death, so the argument goes, the decision to use them carries with it at least the tacit decision to facilitate the patient's death. In rejecting the argument, pain specialists point to their intention. "We are treating pain, and our intentions are to do just that," notes Portenoy. They point out that the compelling need of a particular phase of the disease may be to relieve the patient's symptoms and provide comfort. Patients may still be concerned that the use of drugs to treat their pain could at the same time accelerate their death. This would be true particularly of patients who are not ready to die. The concern often focuses on the danger of overdosing unintentionally or running the risk of toxic side effects. However understandable, the concern is unnecessary, says Portenoy. "Patients should be reassured that when these drugs are used appropriately the side effects they produce are not in themselves lethal." There is plenty of evidence to demonstrate that these therapies do not accelerate death by virtue of their toxic side effects. Compared to anti-inflammatory drugs, which cause damage to the kidneys, and steroids, which compromise the immune system and have other negative effects, opioids generally are far safer.

Even the Vatican's 1980 *Declaration on Euthanasia* makes two unequivocal and notable observations:

> Human and Christian prudence suggest for the majority of sick people the use of medicines capable of alleviating or suppressing pain, even though these may cause as a secondary effect semiconsciousness and reduced lucidity. As for those not in a state to express themselves, one can reasonably presume that they wish to take these painkillers.[3]

The same declaration takes the argument one step further by asking whether religion and morality permit the doctor and the patient to use narcotics to suppress pain and consciousness, even when doing so will shorten life. In its response, the declaration cites Pope Pius XII: "If no other means exist, and if, in the given circumstances, this does not prevent the carrying out of other religious and moral duties: Yes."[4] The justification is derived from the fact that the effective relief of pain is the overriding intention. Under that condition, the risk of death is a reasonable one to take.

The Hastings Center, a non-profit institute for research in bioethics, in its *Guidelines on the Termination of Life-Sustaining Treatment and the Care of the Dying,* has adopted a similar position: "Providing large quantities of narcotic analgesics does not constitute wrongful killing when the purpose is not to shorten the lives of these patients, but to alleviate their pain and suffering."[5] This position assumes a careful evaluation of alternative

ways of relieving the pain and a decision that the administration
of pain-killing drugs in large quantities is in the best interests of
the patient. The Hastings Center guidelines conclude, "There are
no sound moral grounds for failing to provide adequate relief
from pain to those who are dying and wish such relief."[6]

WHAT DOCTORS CAN DO

In practical terms, what can someone who is drawing up advance
medical directives for pain management reasonably expect of caregivers? According to the World Health Organization (WHO), effective pain management should always be available to the patient.
In its 1983 position paper on the use of drug therapy for severe
pain in terminal illness, the American College of Physicians con-
curs, dismissing fears of addiction as meaningless. "Although fear
of patients becoming dependent on narcotics has limited the effective use of morphine and other narcotic drugs, such fear is unfounded because dependence is of little consequence in the context
of terminal illness."[7] This position paper went on to say that physicians should remain flexible in treating the severe, chronic pain in
terminal illness, adjusting the dosage, the frequency, and the route
of application to the needs of the patient.

Echoing that sentiment, Sydney H. Wanzer and his colleagues
wrote in the *New England Journal of Medicine* that the principle of
continually adjusted care is nowhere more important than in the
control of pain, fear, and suffering. "The hopelessly ill patient
must have whatever is necessary to control pain."[8] In their analysis, the authors consider several critical issues. The first is the
widespread belief that physicians do not attend adequately to the
relief of pain. This belief, they contend, is the source of extreme
concern not only for patients but also for their families and the
public at large. "Because of this perceived professional deficiency,
people fear that needless suffering will be allowed to occur as
patients are dying."[9] They conclude that these fears are largely well
founded.

In situations where there is a balance to be drawn between
minimizing pain and suffering and hastening death in a terminally
ill patient, Wanzer and his colleagues have no hesitation in saying

that the balance must be struck in favor of relieving pain by providing the medication in whatever amount and by whatever route is necessary to provide relief. "It is morally correct to increase the dose of narcotics to whatever dose is needed, even though the medication may contribute to the depression of respiration or blood pressure, the dulling of consciousness or even death, provided the primary goal of the physician is to relieve suffering."[10] As they pointedly put it, the proper dose of pain medication is that which relieves pain and suffering adequately, even if it leaves the patient unconscious.

Wanzer and his colleagues also make a number of recommendations in order to address the problem of dying patients who, fearing that their physician will not be available to manage their pain as death approaches, feel abandoned. To anticipate and neutralize this concern, they should be given every reason to believe not only that their physician will be on hand when he or she is needed most, but especially that their pain will be controlled successfully.

Successful pain control depends on a number of factors. When possible, pain medication should be administered orally in the interests of patient autonomy. At the same time, Wanzer and his colleagues recognize that normally, when the patient is near-terminal or actually terminal, it will probably be necessary to deliver the medication directly into the bloodstream. Any rationing of pain medication is wholly unacceptable, and in the case of patients who suffer periodic pain, medication should be taken immediately at the onset of pain. Waiting until the pain is at full force only makes its control more difficult.

Another recommendation is that physicians inform both patients and their families that concerns about addiction are unwarranted. Indeed, they should be told that the effective management of pain will result only in the physical and emotional well-being of the patient.

Few caregivers would disagree in principle with Wanzer's conclusion that allowing patients to endure unbearable pain or suffering is unethical medical practice. Unfortunately, as we have already explained, the management of pain is so poorly understood from a clinical point of view that patients are at serious risk of experiencing great pain. Apart from the unwarranted fear of addiction mentioned earlier, all the evidence suggests that physicians, for example, habitually underestimate the severity of pain or the amount of medication required to deal effectively with a particular patient's level of pain. As we said before, the best protection for patients and their families lies in being as fully informed as possible about pain management, and in speaking up clearly. In this way, they will know what is possible and can make articulate, specific requests of their doctors.

PAIN AND SUFFERING

Daniel Callahan of the Hastings Center, author of *Setting Limits*, raises another issue.[11] While the means to relieve pain are now readily available—assuming there is the will and the skill to use them—is there much point to maintaining life for long when only massive and continuous pain medication will make that person's life tolerable? In other words, does the possibility of controlling a patient's pain justify prolonging his or her life in an otherwise hopeless illness? A well-drawn living will needs to be clear about the point at which hopelessness becomes more intolerable than pain, and whether in addition to being protected from pain, the patient also wants to be protected from medical interventions that serve only to protract a hopeless situation.

Being clear on this point involves reflection on the distinction between pain and suffering. We can experience intense pain without experiencing any sense of psychological suffering. It is also possible to suffer in the absence of any pain. Pain, then, is not to be confused with suffering any more than the management of the former is to be identified with the relief of the latter. Suffering, according to Callahan, is the reasonable hopelessness people experience when they face the prospect of unending pain or realize that the severity of their illness empties life of any meaning. In these circumstances, Callahan concludes that "a medicine that can only hold out the prospect of prolonging life in order to extend, but not relieve, suffering has come to the end of its resources and purpose."[12]

According to Russell Portenoy, the distinction between pain and suffering must be recognized in order to treat patients properly. But this is not easy to do. "I think the symptom of pain contributes to the suffering of the patient, but suffering can be independent of pain." Portenoy says. As he explains it, suffering is more or less synonymous with impaired quality of life, the global response to numerous losses. In the vast majority of cases pain and other symptoms seem to increase suffering in the patient. But there are other obvious factors. "Patients can have independent psychological disorders like depression or anxiety," he says. Serious, and certainly prolonged, illness brings with it social disruptions in the life of the patient, not to mention family crises, financial worries, premonitions of death, and the concerns that arise from the manifestation of new symptoms and their possible significance. Developments like these can seriously limit a patient's ability to work or pursue personal interests. "All of these things contribute to the patient's suffering or impairment of the patient's quality of life," Portenoy says.

These observations have important implications. Concentrating on physical pain as if it were the sole concern in a patient who is actually experiencing what Portenoy describes as suffering may well result in a patient who is more comfortable, but no less distressed. Indeed, there are some patients who suffer serious depression once their pain has been alleviated. Even more curious is a small body of evidence suggesting that some patients enjoy a better quality of life because of, not despite, their pain. It may be that the presence of pain distracts people so that they can overlook the reality of their disease. It may also be that pain brings patients closer emotionally to their family. Another possible explanation is that pain serves to focus and confine anxiety or depression by directing the patient's attention elsewhere. In such cases, if the pain is removed, the patient may begin to suffer. Portenoy believes that the explanations so far advanced to explain the phenomenon are inadequate. "But the phenomenon is observed; not everybody feels better when you take away their pain," he says. Such an observation "tells the doctor that he has to look at the larger issue of suffering and the various components of that experience." For instance, it may be wrong to try to convince patients that with the elimination or control of the symptom, they will be able to function better or cope more adequately. In reality, none of this may be true.

PAIN CONTROL AND SEDATION

Controlling pain and maintaining alertness are not necessarily incompatible. The patient should not, according to Portenoy, believe that intensive pain therapy is automatically going to turn him into a "zombie." "The idea is not to produce analgesia by anesthetizing the person, thereby creating a degree of sedation incompatible with function. The idea is to produce analgesia with retention of function to the extent that the patient wants that."

Nevertheless, sedation can be a problem. This is particularly true in the case of dying patients who are being treated with opioid drugs. Part of the problem may stem from a failure to realize that sedation can be caused by things other than drugs. The disease itself could be affecting the activity of the brain. Dehydration and electrolyte disturbances can also contribute to the sedation of a patient. Doctors and nurses, as well as patients and their families, should therefore guard against a tendency to view opioid drugs—since they are stigmatized drugs—as if they were the only cause of sedation.

Take, for example, the case of patients who, diagnosed with multiple brain metastases, become sedated on an opioid drug. They may improve for a while if the drug therapy is stopped; but because of the metastases, they will not resume normal cognitive functions, and their headaches will return. Under circumstances where there are other major causes of the patients' sedation and confusion, any decision to abandon the use of opioids may be quite unreasonable.

Further complicating the issue of sedation and patient alertness and control is the apparently subliminal fear that sedation resulting from opioid drug therapy is irreversible. Like the fear of addiction discussed earlier, this is unfounded. As the dosage of such a drug is increased, the patient may become sedated. But the doctor can decrease the dosage or stop it altogether, just as he or she might stop using an antihypertensive or antibiotic; and the sedation, if indeed caused by the opioid, would stop.

The fact that opioid-induced sedation is reversible may, paradoxically, create its own difficulties, more for the family and the clinicians caring for the patients than for the patients themselves. People who have gone to the trouble of preparing a living will or appointing a proxy are signaling their interest in controlling decisions about their medical care. When in the course of pain therapy they become sedated, they are not able to remain in control. Members of the family and clinicians now find themselves making medical decisions based on the word of the proxy or the content of the living will, which has become operative only as a result of a reversible condition. The perplexing question that now arises is whether the patient who has become unable to make decisions would want the condition reversed to retain immediate control or continue to be sedated and free of pain. Since there is a real choice here, it is preferable if the patient can remain alert enough, or be allowed to become temporarily alert, in order to choose.

Decisions to resuscitate a patient are often based on the quality of life that might remain for the patient. If the doctors see that the only result of pain therapy is sedation and an inability to function, they may lean toward not resuscitating. Often the decision will be based on the stage of the disease. "If the patient is in a relatively early stage of disease," says Portenoy, "then no matter what the setting, the doctors will recognize that a drug is a big problem for that patient, and they will use whatever they have available to them, including very invasive procedures, to relieve the pain, reduce drug dosage, and allow the patient to be more functional." This question becomes less clear in the case of a patient whose disease is far advanced.

According to Portenoy, some good options are not always available, depending upon how well equipped the hospital and how skilled the staff in pain management. In the case of a patient, for instance, with severe pain in the lower abdomen, the use of an epidural catheter (pain medication fed directly into the tissue in the spinal column) might bring great relief. But not every hospital is equipped and skilled in this technique. Instead, the only relief will come from drugs accompanied by terrible side effects, sedation, and confusion.

Knowing that options are available, a doctor who does not have them available or know how to use them may be in an extremely uncomfortable position. For example, in treating a patient who is severely sedated with opioid drugs against progressively unbearable pain, the doctor might like to put an epidural catheter in place. But he or she may not because there is no anesthesiologist to assist. And even with the assistance to complete the procedure, the doctor may feel uncomfortable about increasing the drug dosage because of a lack of experience.

In those situations, the possibility of conflict between family members and clinicians increases. The focus of the conflict is sedation, and the concern is either that not enough is being done to control the patient's pain or that too much is being done, threatening his or her ability to function. Family members may insist that the patient be kept alert because "there is a lot more to talk about," or "we need to be clear about what Dad wants us to do." In response, the doctor might say that allowing the patient to become more alert would cause unbearable pain to return. On the other hand, while the clinician has grave concerns about sedating the patient too severely, the only concern of the family might be to make the patient comfortable. In some situations the doctors might point out to the family that if the patient were less sleepy, he or she could return home and enjoy being with the family. But members of the family, observing that they have already lived through three months of terrible pain, declare that they will not let that happen to the patient again. Clearly there is no simple answer as patients, their family, and their doctors work to find an acceptable balance between the benefits and the unacceptable side effects of sedation. Early discussions between patients and physicians will go a long way toward creating that balance. Patients should ask things like, "Is the goal of pain therapy comfort without limiting my mental or physical functions?" "Would you be prepared to change my pain therapy, if I cannot stay alert?" "What other kinds of pain therapy are available if the normal procedures don't work?" "Can you keep me comfortable, without turning me into a zombie?"

Another critical question for the patient is how the doctor is going to regard a living will if sedation from pain therapy medications is causing incompetence. If the patient is close to death, it would not be unusual for a doctor to assume that the patient's incompetence is irreversible and for that reason be unwilling to allow any further suffering. In that case, the contents of an advance medical directive would prevail. But other doctors could respond quite differently. Since, as we said, sedation is reversible, they might say that even if death is imminent, they want to know as directly as possible what the patient wants. For this reason they are prepared to do whatever is necessary to rouse the patient for a time. Although most clinicians lean toward the first response, it cannot be assumed in every case. For this reason Portenoy's suggestion is worth remembering: "I do think a very knowledgeable patient might say to his doctor, 'At what point would you consider my advance directive to be operative if you believed my incompetence was related to pain therapy and therefore reversible, but at a price?' "

NOTES

1. Russell K. Portenoy, interview with authors, January 1991. All subsequent quotations from Dr. Portenoy cited in this chapter are from this interview.
2. Ronald Melzack, "The Tragedy of Needless Pain," *Scientific American,* February 1990, 27–33.
3. Vatican, *Declaration on Euthanasia, Sacred Congregation for Doctrine of the Faith* (Rome, 1980), 6.
4. Ibid., 7.
5. Hastings Center, *Guidelines on the Termination of Life-Sustaining Treatment and the Care of the Dying* (Briarcliff Manor, N.Y.: Hastings Center, 1987), 73.
6. Ibid., 73.
7. "Drug Therapy for Severe Chronic Pain in Terminal Illness," *Annals of Internal Medicine* 99 (December 1983), 870–73.
8. Sydney H. Wanzer et al., "The Physician's Responsibility toward Hopelessly Ill Patients," *New England Journal of Medicine* 320 (30 March 1989), 844–849.
9. Ibid.
10. Ibid.
11. Daniel Callahan, *Setting Limits* (New York: Simon and Schuster, 1987), 177.
12. Ibid., 178.

SEVEN

The Challenge
of Suicide

*That a person can know when to die and can die at will, intentionally, with
full awareness of what he is doing, is a concept so alien to our culture that
one scarcely dares mention it without an apology.*

ROBERT S. DE ROPP
The Master Game

"There is but one serious philosophical problem," wrote the
French novelist and philosopher Albert Camus, "and that is suicide. Judging whether life is or is not worth living amounts to
answering the fundamental question of philosophy."[1] For most of
us, Camus's words sound overdramatized and remote from the
routines and demands of everyday experience. But for anyone
faced with the pain, uncertainty, and loss of control that often
accompany a terminal illness, Camus's observations suddenly become all too relevant. For the dying patient, questions about
refusing, continuing, or terminating treatment are always questions about whether or not life, in its present form, is worth living.
Given this reality, it would be irresponsible to discuss planning for
the end of life and not treat suicide as a real and familiar option
for many terminally ill patients.

THE TWO EXTREMES

Debates and publications about terminal care unfortunately pay
little attention to suicide as an option for dying patients. In fact,

when suicide is mentioned at all, it is usually to reassure the listener or reader that treatment refusal or removal decisions are no longer equated with suicide by most judges, lawmakers, or medical personnel.[2] The option of suicide itself—in relation to the law, to the role of institutions and caregivers, and to the needs and wishes of patients—is routinely ignored. When suicide is discussed, it is often in an abstract manner detached from the experiences and testimonies of terminally ill patients and others with reasons to explore the option of self-inflicted death. Usually, these discussions hover toward one of two extremes.

In one camp are those who insist that the act of taking one's own life is always wrong, regardless of the circumstances. Proponents of this view may appeal to any number of arguments: moral (suicide is evil), religious (suicide is sinful), psychological (the desire to take one's life is irrational), legal (layers of precedents against suicide exist), or social (suicide is against the interests of the family and society as a whole). The most extreme statement of this position is expressed by psychiatrist Erwin Reigel. "Suicide cannot really be 'chosen,' " writes Dr. Reigel, "since an intense overwhelmingly inner compulsion renders any free 'choice' null and void. . . . No one is ever . . . 100 percent suicidal—no human being, no matter how determined he or she may seem to be to put an end to life, does not somewhere cherish the hope of being saved."[3]

In the other camp are those who argue that control over one's own destiny—deciding whether or not one will continue to live, as well as how, when, and where one will die—is a basic human right. Members of this group, including such very active organizations as the Hemlock Society, may also point to moral arguments, religious and philosophical tradition, psychology, and natural law to support their stance. We can discuss circumstances, causes, and motivations and appeal to religion, morality, and law until we're blue in the face, the defenders of this view insist. But when all is said and done, every person, regardless of the circumstances, has the fundamental right to end his or her own life at a time and place and in a manner of his or her own choosing. The psychiatrist Thomas Szasz goes so far in his unequivocal advocacy of a person's right to commit suicide that he rejects the word *suicide* itself as an unacknowledged pejorative, suggesting instead that self-killing, "should be called 'suicide' only by those who disapprove of it; and should be called 'death control' by those who approve of it."[4]

While neither of these positions spends much time describing the actual experiences of terminally ill patients, the question of suicide for the terminally ill is central to both. For those who disapprove of suicide, the prolongation of painful, humiliating terminal illness represents the agonizing extreme to which the value and sanctity of human life must be affirmed and protected, regardless of the expressed desires of the patient to end his or her life. For those who approve, on the other hand, suicide and terminal illness go hand in hand, the former described as such a potentially rational response to the latter that it seems almost inevitable, again apart from the desires and motivations of any particular patient. The proponents of neither position appear daunted by the tenuous, constantly shifting situations in which dying patients are forced to live and communicate, or the uncertainty and ambivalence in which end-of-life decisions are often made. Although Szasz acknowledges that suicide is often considered as an option by those who are desperate and confused, he goes on to make the reassuring, but clinically insupportable, claim that all serious, confidently intended suicide attempts succeed, while those that are confused or misdirected invariably fail—once again without reference to the testimonies and experiences of patients themselves.[5]

It would be a great relief if such a difficult and troubling issue could be treated so simply and confidently: suicide should either always be prevented because the desire to take one's life is finally impossible and therefore always against the patient's real interest, or, conversely, always be advocated because attempts to the contrary are both unjust and ineffective—those who wish it will inevitably succeed, and those who don't will fail. Unfortunately, this is rarely the case. Persons confronted with a terminal illness often think of suicide as one of their options. And faced with the day-to-day realities of their illness and the system of personal and professional relationships through which their care is provided, they rarely view their situations with the same clarity or conviction as the champions of either of these extremist positions.

AVOIDING THE QUESTION

In a curious way, the failure of doctors to discuss suicide openly as an option for dying patients can be traced, at least in part, to the success of the patients' rights movement during the past twenty years. In response to the challenges of patients and their families, judges, lawmakers, and hospital administrators have increasingly come to question the necessity of treatments and technology that can only prolong life without improving the patient's condition. This questioning of the usefulness and humanity of various treatments in cases involving terminal illness has been the rationale behind many, if not most, decisions to withdraw or withhold treatment. Convinced that their decisions are in response to the wisdom of a particular treatment—and not a patient's wish to die—doctors have become more and more open to requests to forego life-sustaining care. In such cases, death, if and when it comes, is understood to result from the disease process itself or the injury to the patient, and not the decision to remove or forego treatment. As we saw earlier, this distinction helped pave the way for acceptance of decisions to forego treatment.

More often than not, this approach has been carried to the point that the patient's motivations in refusing treatment are confused with those of the doctor: "In cases of refusing treatment, it is not that the patient wants to die, but rather that the patient does not want to undergo a certain treatment and is willing to accept death as a consequence of that decision."[6] Understandably and appropriately, patients have been advised and instructed to state their wishes—whether in preparing living wills, instructing surrogates, or responding to the questions of their caregivers—in terms that comply with the criteria of natural death legislation and institutional policy. But patients' decisions to forego treatment, even when made in advance, are rarely based on a detached appraisal of particular technologies or treatment protocols. For the patient or future patient, the question is usually, Do I, or would I, wish to continue living in this condition? And the distinction between suicide and foregoing treatment is not nearly as convincing or reassuring to the patient wishing to die as it is to the clinician critically appraising a treatment's chance of success, or wishing to protect himself or herself from any threat of civil, criminal, or professional liability.

Given this situation, it is easy to see how and why questions regarding suicide have often been swept under the rug, even as terminally ill patients are becoming increasingly empowered to make their own decisions about the treatments they will or will not receive.

SUICIDE AND THE LAW

Under English common law, suicide and attempted suicide, regardless of the circumstances that precipitated them, were treated as terrible crimes against God, nature, and society. In his openly sympathetic treatment of suicide among literary figures, *The Savage God,* English literary critic Alfred Alvarez graphically describes the punishment of one failed suicide attempt in nineteenth-century London:

> A man was hanged who had cut his throat, but who had been brought back to life. They hanged him for suicide. The doctor had warned them that it was impossible to hang him as the throat would burst open and he would breathe through the aperture. They did not listen to his advice and hanged their man. The wound in the neck immediately opened and the man came back to life again although he was hanged. It took time to convoke the aldermen to decide the question of what was to be done. At length the aldermen assembled and bound up the neck below the wound until he died.[7]

Often, however, the punishment didn't end with the victim's death. Suicide was considered so heinous a crime that the persecution of the offender extended to the treatment of the body after death. "As recently as 1823," writes psychiatrist Herbert Hendin, in the United States, "a suicide's body was buried at midnight at a crossroad with a stake driven through the body and a stone placed over the face."[8]

In a society like our own, where the free will, and not the body of the individual, is the subject of the law and—except in the most extreme cases—the object of its retribution, it no longer makes sense to threaten a person considering suicide with punishment by death. Consequently, criminal legislation regarding suicide has become progressively more liberal. And in America, where the severities of English common law were never fully applied, suicide itself is no longer a crime in any legislative jurisdiction. Curiously, attempted suicide is still against the law in a few places, but such laws have rarely been enforced, with the last recorded prosecution having taken place more than thirty years ago.[9]

The fact that suicide and attempted suicide have been largely decriminalized in our society does not, however, signal suicide's social and legal acceptance, or even tolerance. Lawmakers and law enforcers have abandoned the criminal prosecution and punishment of suicide, not because they have come to regard ending one's life as a potentially sane and responsible option for each citizen, but simply because such measures have proven contradictory and ineffective. While we have abandoned the use of criminal law to ban self-killing, we have as a society given active encouragement and legal support to the efforts of concerned groups, often with a vested interest—notably medical, psycho-therapeutic, and religious institutions and insurance companies—to diagnose, discourage, and prevent suicide. Rather than violently suppress the contradictions involved in the prevention of suicide, as our ancestors tried to do, we have institutionalized them, simultaneously treating suicide as a right of the individual and the prevention of suicide as an interest of society at large. While it may be perfectly legal to kill oneself, the suspicion that that is one's intention is usually grounds not only for persuasive intervention, but even involuntary incarceration for "treatment and observation."

Recently, many of the suicide-prevention initiatives have been shown to be largely ineffective. The more drastic measures, such as involuntary incarceration, may actually exacerbate the problem, with disturbed persons sometimes attempting to commit suicide rather than risk returning to an institution. In response to this, many physicians and therapists have abandoned such measures, and laws and policies are currently being reformed to respect the rights of even potentially suicidal patients.[10] Most of the ambivalence and conflict concerning the rights of the patient and the interest of society with regard to suicide is now seen in society at large, and not in the professional community, which is increasingly held accountable for its contradictions through the constraints of civil and criminal law, as well as peer review. Even sympathetic physicians or therapists may feel compelled to intervene, not simply from the threat of medical review or criminal prosecution for negligence, but from the fear of being sued by bereaved family members or even clients themselves, when suicide attempts prove unsuccessful.

In order to understand current law and policy on suicide for the terminally ill, it is important to know how and why legislators, judges, and policymakers have consistently distinguished between ending one's life through suicide and withholding or withdrawing life-sustaining treatment.

As we saw, for many people on both sides of the issue the two are essentially the same. For those who oppose a patient's right to terminate treatment, either the decision to refuse treatments or the decision to take an overdose of drugs results in death and therefore constitutes suicide (for those who make the decision) or murder (for those who provide assistance). "In any discussion of euthanasia," writes former U.S. Surgeon General C. Everett Koop, "an understanding of terminology is essential. The deliberate killing of one human being by another, no matter what the motivation might be, is murder."[11] Koop goes on to acknowledge that in discussions of euthanasia, distinctions are sometimes made between active killing and letting die, a distinction he is unwilling to make himself.

Others who support this general view are hesitant to equate suicide and terminating treatment, but they still see the two as connected in very troubling ways. While they might see the right of a particular patient to refuse unwarranted treatment as morally, legally, and medically defensible in and of itself, they fear that allowing it in one case might lead to the eventual acceptance of other undesirable options, such as suicide, in the future. "If active killing of the suffering would lead to active killing of others," writes ethicist Robert Veatch in describing the advocates of this position, "that is of a relevant consequence, which must be taken into account in evaluating even the first, most apparently justifiable act of this sort [i.e., withdrawing or withholding treatment]."[12]

Ironically, many who support suicide and the termination of treatment as options use basically the same arguments—preserving dignity, making the most humane choice, acting morally—as their opponents, but in support of very different conclusions. The supporters say, If patients should be allowed to determine their own course of treatment, shouldn't they also be allowed—when all treatment options appear futile and the only thing that lies ahead is a painful, lingering death—to take the steps necessary to end their lives with dignity? Doesn't support for the withholding or withdrawal of life-sustaining treatment lead inevitably, and humanely, to support for the option of assisted suicide? "What, morally," argues ethicist Joseph Fletcher, "is the difference between doing nothing to keep a patient alive and giving a fatal dose of a pain-killing or other legal drug?" The end or purpose of both, Fletcher insists, "is exactly the same: to contrive or bring about the patient's death."[13]

Many of us may find one of these two arguments thoughtful and persuasive. What is useful to know, however, in facing the issues in one's life is how our courts, legislators, and health-care institutions have responded to the question. The fact is that, for the past twenty years, lawmakers, judges, and institutional policy-makers have consistently refused to treat suicide and withholding or withdrawing treatment as if they were the same thing. In fact, opinions and rulings have, time and time again, upheld the conviction that the two are totally different.

The New Jersey Supreme Court's decision in the *Quinlan* case was based in part on this very distinction. In that groundbreaking case, the judges ruled that, in situations where accident or disease has rendered persons incapable of continuing life on their own, the cause of death, when it comes, is the accident or disease process itself, not the withdrawal of treatment. According to the court's decision, "There is a real and in this case determinative distinction between the unlawful taking of the life of another and the ending of artificial life-support systems as a matter of self-determination."[14] It is this distinction that many judges and administrators have had in mind when defending a decision to allow treatment to be withheld or removed as "putting matters in God's hands" or "letting nature take its course."

Another argument in support of the distinction between suicide and foregoing treatment is that the desired end of the action in withholding or withdrawal cases is simply the removal of unwanted treatment, not necessarily the immediate death of the patient. This was dramatized in the case of Karen Quinlan, who remained alive in her coma for almost nine years after her doctors slowly and carefully weaned her from her respirator.

Consequently, in those cases where care is foregone or discontinued, death is interpreted as resulting from accident or disease, not from the patient's or proxy's decision or the caregiver's action. In cases involving suicide, on the other hand, death is ruled to be the direct result of the actions of the patient and anyone else who may have helped. This is true regardless of the extent of the injury or disease, or the nearness of death. Even if death from disease or injury is thought to have been only hours or even minutes away, death in reported cases of suicide is always ruled to be the result of the action of the patient and those providing assistance, not of the previous physical condition.

This legal and medical distinction between suicide and refusing treatment has, of course, had a liberalizing effect on court decisions, natural death legislation, and hospital policy toward the withholding and withdrawal of treatment. If the refusal of care will not be recorded as the *cause* of a patient's death, doctors and hospitals will usually be much more responsive to the wishes of patients who, for whatever reason, decide to forego treatment.

The very same distinction has had an opposite, completely negative effect for advocates of a patient's right to commit suicide, as well as for patients for whom the withholding or withdrawal of treatment fails to provide the relief they desire. But the distinction itself does not necessarily imply that the health-care community is unsympathetic to the desire of terminally ill patients to take their own lives.

Many of those who refuse to acknowledge a person's *right* to take his or her own life are willing to concede that in certain cases involving terminal illness suicide may sometimes be considered a sane, responsible decision. In his recent study entitled *Suicide in America,* Herbert Hendin decries the uncritical "glorification of suicide" by the media and many right-to-die groups. Nevertheless, he says:

> We need not argue the issue of whether it is rational for an individual with a painful terminal illness to refuse extraordinary life-saving measures or to arrange more actively to end his life. Most would agree it is, and that is precisely why supporters of the "right to suicide" or "death control" position are constantly presenting the case of a patient suffering from incurable, painful cancer as the case on which they based their arguments.[15]

For the opposite reasons, as we saw, many of those who oppose a patient's right to suicide even in situations involving painful terminal illness do so not because they question the sanity of the act itself but because they fear that, in acknowledging the right to suicide in this special case, they might inadvertently contribute to its more general acceptance and support. Nevertheless, Hendin's point remains: most people will acknowledge, at least in principle, a terminally ill patient's right to end his or her life, especially in cases involving severe pain or disability. What people have more trouble agreeing about is the question of how, where, and, especially, with whose assistance the patient's wishes are to be honored.

PHYSICIAN-ASSISTED SUICIDE

The arguments for and against physician-assisted suicide for the terminally ill are now familiar from a flood of articles and broadcasts. The key to all the arguments, on both sides of the issue, is the unique role that the physician plays in our society. To those who favor physician-assisted suicide, the question is simple and straightforward: Who could be a more appropriate choice than physicians, with their intimate knowledge of their patient's condition, as well as their knowledge of and easy access to the most effective and humane methods of ending life?

On the other side of the issue are those who question the wisdom of appointing the physician, whose self-declared and socially expected role has always been the healing of illness and sustaining of life, as the person who would also be responsible for terminating life. The advocates of this position argue, Wouldn't such a dramatic shift in or confusion of responsibilities erode the trust and confidence of patients?

In addition to the role conflict involved in assisting suicide, many physicians who oppose assisting suicide also appeal directly to the sacred and official documents of their tradition. Many lean on what some consider a questionable interpretation of the Hippocratic Oath, which says that physicians "will neither give a deadly drug to anybody if asked for it, nor . . . make a suggestion to this effect."[16] Others rely on a special report of the Judicial Council of the American Medical Association, which states unequivocally, "The intentional termination of the life of one human being by another—mercy killing—is contrary to that for which the medical profession stands and is contrary to the policy of the American Medical Association."[17]

Perhaps the most persuasive argument against physician-assisted suicide is the stubborn resistance of the medical community itself, apart from any particular argument or defense. One recent study indicated that most physicians (at least two out of three)—even many of those sympathetic to the wishes of suicidal patients—would continue to refuse to provide assistance even if such a practice was legally allowed and endorsed by their institutions and professional associations.[18] Anthropologist Margaret Mead, explaining why she drew up what was arguably one of the first advance health-care directives, insisted that her document was designed to protect both herself (from treatment she did not desire) and her potential caregiver (from being forced to act in a manner inconsistent with his or her values).[19] It seems unlikely that the medical profession will ever allow itself to be dragged involuntarily into euthanasia for the terminally ill. Professor Leon Kass, of the University of Chicago, points out the right to be mercifully killed implies a duty to kill, which is unlikely to be accepted by physicians.[20]

Meanwhile, assisted suicide is, in any case, against the law, although no uniform guidelines remain for what class of crime it is or how it should be prosecuted. Currently, the states are evenly divided among those that treat it as manslaughter, those that treat it as a separate offense altogether, and those that provide no separate definition, leaving it to the courts' judgment to treat it as anything from homicide to a less severe crime.[21] But in all fifty states assisting suicide is treated as a serious criminal offense, and—true to our societal ambivalence about the issue—rarely, if ever, prosecuted. Most laws, as currently written and enforced, serve as an effective deterrent to *acknowledgment* of the practice of assisted suicide, not to its actual occurrence. It could be argued that such is the law's intent.

Where does all of this leave patients wishing to end their lives and caregivers, family, or friends willing to assist them? Unfortunately, it leaves them where they have always been—cooperating in secret, outside the endorsement or review of law and institutions, and with frightfully little help or attention given to the situation by legislators, the medical profession, or health-care institutions.

THE ONGOING DEBATE

Two recent cases have brought the issue to the headlines but have done little to suggest a solution to the problem. First and most spectacular was the 1990 murder trial and acquittal of Jack Kevorkian, the Michigan physician who helped Alzheimer's patient Janet Atkins to an easy death with his now-infamous suicide machine, a device designed to allow the patient to self-administer pain-relieving sedatives and a lethal dose of barbiturates. Kevorkian, with his unorthodox behavior and failure to provide his client with even the most perfunctory examination or diagnosis, was easy prey to those who oppose physician assistance, and the more troubling issues raised by the case were generally ignored by both the media and the medical profession. Since that time, Dr. Kevorkian has assisted two more patients in ending their lives, and the outcome of these cases is undetermined as of this writing.

Harder for most to ignore was the candid and painful testimony of Dr. Timothy Quill of Rochester, New York, in the *New England Journal of Medicine*.[22] Quill managed for months to defer the questions of his client Diane, a middle-aged leukemia patient whom he had attended for more than eight years, about what she would do when her condition deteriorated to the point that she no longer wished to endure it. But when Diane herself finally determined that the time had come, Quill reluctantly prescribed a potentially lethal dose of barbiturates, with a clear, if never fully acknowledged understanding that she intended to use the drugs to take her own life. At first, Quill did what he insists that most of his colleagues do under similar circumstances: he reported the cause of death as leukemia. Only later did he come forward to declare his actions publically.

Throughout the article, Quill never claims that his actions represent an appropriate or model response for physicians faced with similar situations, nor does he propose a particular legal or institutional response to the problem. What he does suggest is that physicians more openly acknowledge to their patients and themselves the circumstances in which terminal care is commonly provided and received, and the conflicts and dilemmas that often arise for anyone involved in end-of-life decision making. "Although I know we have measures to help control pain and lessen suffering," he declares, "to think that people do not suffer in the process of dying is an illusion. Prolonged dying can occasionally be peaceful, but more often the role of the physician and family is limited to lessening but not eliminating severe pain."[23] For many patients, even unrelievable suffering and pain are meaningful or at least something to be endured. For patients like Diane, however, they represent an indignity from which one must seek release. "Her belief," explained Dr. Quill, "was that it was outrageous that our society wouldn't allow people to end their lives in a humane way."[24]

Some have predicted that the continued failure by the medical community to find a workable solution to the problem of intractable or untreated pain and the desire of many terminal patients to end their lives sooner, will one day result in the public demand that physicians practice euthanasia. But, as we argued earlier, in spite of public opinion to the contrary (almost 60 percent of the population affirm the dying patient's right to assisted suicide),[25] because of physicians themselves and how they view their special role, such a change seems extremely unlikely, at least in the foreseeable future.

A more probable outcome will be a long-overdue examination of some of the more frequent causes of suicide. There may also be more discussion of and money allocated for research in pain management, rehabilitative medicine, care for the elderly, and universal access to care. Most importantly, for our discussion, there may be greater patient control of treatments at the end of life and of the decision-making process.

For most terminally ill patients, many of whom may at some point consider suicide, even such an evasive institutional response would nevertheless be a godsend, greatly reducing the stress, discomfort, and uncertainty of their final days. For those others—for whom the miracles of medical technology and its withdrawal fail to provide relief—the continued legal and institutional neglect of the problem of suicide represents a genuine tragedy, for which no solution is in sight. The widespread sales of a book called *Final Exit,* by Derek Humphry of the Hemlock Society,[26] and the growth in that organization's membership testify to the strength of public interest in the problem, and to the agony of the questions remaining unanswered.

It may well be that Camus's question ultimately lies beyond institutions. Physicians and other caregivers are no better equipped than anyone else to answer the suicidal patient's frequent and penetrating question, "What would you do in my situation?" Finally, we must each answer the question for ourselves of whether or not life is worth living.

And yet, however private and personal the answer to such difficult questions, they can rarely be pondered or deliberated in isolation. As patients increasingly choose the hospital as the place where they will die—or have it chosen for them—the questions that were once absorbed by the circle of family, friends, and the religious community have entered health-care institutions and the public domain, however reluctantly received. "I wonder how many families and physicians secretly help patients over the edge into death in the face of such severe suffering," writes Dr. Quill. "I wonder how many severely ill or dying patients secretly take their lives, dying alone in despair."[27] Until patients, family members, and caregivers are allowed and encouraged to wonder aloud about the issue of suicide, we will never know the answer to these questions, nor will we move any closer to a solution that is both responsible and humane.

NOTES

1. Albert Camus, *The Myth of Sisyphus,* trans. Justin O'Brien (New York: Vintage Books, 1955), 3.
2. President's Commission for the Study of Ethical Problems in Medicine and Biomedical Research, *Deciding to Forego Life-Sustaining Treatment* (Washington, D.C.: Government Printing Office, 1983), 38–39.
3. Erwin Reigel, "Suicide Prevention and the Value of Human Life," in *Suicide: The Philosophical Issues,* M. Pabst Battin and David J. Mayo (New York: St. Martin's, 1980), 206.
4. Thomas S. Szasz, *The Second Sin* (Garden City, N.Y.: Anchor Books, 1974), 75–76.
5. Thomas S. Szasz, "The Ethics of Suicide," in *Suicide: The Philosophical Issues,* ed. M. Pabst Battin and David J. Mayo (New York: St. Martin's, 1980), 186.
6. George J. Annas, *The Rights of Patients* (Carbondale and Edwardsville: Southern Illinois University Press, 1989), 204.
7. Alfred Alvarez, *The Savage God* (New York: Random House, 1973), 1.
8. Herbert Hendin, *Suicide in America* (New York and London: W. W. Norton, 1982), 22.
9. President's Commission, *Deciding to Forego,* 37.
10. Hendin, *Suicide in America.* 194–204.
11. C. Everett Koop, "The Right to Die: The Moral Dilemma," in *Euthanasia,* ed. Robert M. Baird and Stuart E. Rosenbaum (Buffalo, N.Y.: Prometheus Books, 1989), 69–83.
12. Robert M. Veatch, *Death, Dying, and the Biological Revolution* (New Haven and London: Yale University Press, 1989), 67.
13. Baird and Rosenbaum, *Euthanasia,* 94.
14. *In re Quinlan,* 70 N.J. 10, 355 A.2d 647 (1976).
15. Hendin, *Suicide in America,* 214.
16. Veatch, *Death, Dying,* 83.
17. Quoted in Baird and Rosenbaum, *Euthanasia,* 11.
18. Annas, *The Rights of Patients,* 219.
19. Margaret Mead, "The Cultural Shaping of the Ethical Context," in *Who Shall Live? Medicine, Technology, Ethics,* ed. Kenneth Vaux (Philadelphia: Fortress Press, 1970), 10.
20. David Hendin, *Death as a Fact of Life* (New York and London: W. W. Norton, 1984), 85.
21. Leslie Pickering Francis, "Assisting Suicide," in *Suicide: The Philosophical Issues,* ed. M. Pabst Battin and David J. Mayo (New York: St. Martin's, 1980), 256.
22. Timothy E. Quill, "Death and Dignity: A Case of Individualized Decision Making," *New England Journal of Medicine* 324 (7 March 1991), 694.
23. Quoted in *New York Times,* 7 March 1991, A, 1:1.

24. Ibid.
25. Annas, *The Rights of Patients,* 219.
26. Derek Humphry, *Final Exit* (Eugene, Oreg.: Hemlock Society, 1991).
    The Hemlock Society's address is: P.O. Box 11830, Eugene, OR 97440.
27. Quill, "Death and Dignity," 694.

EIGHT

Religious Traditions and the Right to Die

Death is swallowed up in victory.
I CORINTHIANS 15:54

Then will your graves, gethsemani, give up their angels.
THOMAS MERTON

A time to be born, and a time to die.
ECCLESIASTES 3:2

All life is life after death.
PHILIP KAPLEAU

DEATH IN THE PROTESTANT TRADITION

For most of us, the Protestant tradition is associated with the freedom of the individual—and rightly so. At the heart of Protestant theology and practice—from the great works of Martin Luther and John Calvin to the simplest Quaker meeting—is the principle that only God is worthy of the believer's worship, ultimate respect, and obedience. Following closely from this great "Protestant principle" is the conviction that no external authority may come between the individual believer and the God revealed in Jesus Christ. In spite of the undeniable importance of law, civil and church governments, charismatic leadership, and the biblical witness for the Protestant faith, nothing finally has priority over the individual and his or her own conscience in relation to God. Luther, in fact, equated the "truth of the Gospel" and the individual's "freedom of conscience in Christ." According to the great Reformation theologian, these are "not to be jeopardized on the basis of anybody's name or title, regardless of how great he may be, even if he were an apostle or an angel from heaven."[1]

Protestant individualism and freedom of conscience have had an enormous and ongoing impact on the social and political context in which we view issues of justice, life, and death. From the Baptist minister Roger Williams's call for religious tolerance and freedom of conscience in colonial America, to the Bill of Rights, all the way to our present-day patients' rights movement, Protestants have traditionally thought of themselves as champions of the individual in relation to governments and other institutions, supporting the rights of each one of us to hold our own unique beliefs and values and to make our own choices about the things that affect our lives. And although no mainline Protestant tradition has ever fully embodied Williams's prescription that "God's people were and ought to be Nonconformitants,"[2] most have consistently tried to support the rights of those who are.

Unfortunately for our discussion here, anyone seeking a definitive word on the "Protestant position" on any moral or political issue—or general guidelines to follow in any process of ethical decision making—is likely to be confused and disappointed. The Protestant tradition, having done much to give us the right to make our own choices, has done far less to help us deal with the problems and complexities involved in actually making those choices. In contrast, quick glance at the work of any significant twentieth-century Catholic theologian, such as Karl Rahner, will reveal numerous attempts to address the complexities of medical care and end-of-life decision making, written for the actual edification and instruction of individual Catholics and with broad applicability across the Catholic community. This cannot be said for the work of any major twentieth-century Protestant theologian, and—with the notable exception of Karl Barth—most Protestant theologians have ignored the issue completely.

That's the bad news for Protestants. The good news is that there is much within the Protestant tradition that can help individual Protestants, especially at the present time. As we have discussed at length, recent advances in medical care and technology have resulted in new treatment options, and with them new decisions and dilemmas for caregivers, patients, and their family and friends. In light of this, many traditional formulas for decision making and definitions of life and death now seem rigid and unsatisfying. For Protestants, the scene is a familiar one. In many ways, making difficult decisions and building consensus in the midst of diversity, without the benefit of any absolute authority, is a legacy of Protestantism.

The Priesthood of Every Believer

In the Protestant tradition, the doctrine of the priesthood of every believer was the outgrowth of Luther's rejection of the very idea of a professional clergy, uniquely qualified to interpret the scripture, lead worship, and administer the sacraments. Instead of a system of experts, above the challenge or reproach of the laity, Luther called for all Christians to serve as priests to one another, providing guidance, support, and discipline, according to their various skills, talents, and experience. "Therefore every one who knows that he is a Christian," insisted Luther, "should be fully assured that all of us alike are priests, and that we all have the same authority in regard to the word and the sacraments."[3]

The important thing to remember here is that, in Luther's doctrine, no one served as a priest to himself or herself. Luther did not simply replace a handful of experts, each responsible for the

spiritual needs of all the members of his parish, with a church full
of experts, each responsible only for his or her own needs, apart
from the strengths and frailties of everyone else. Instead, he challenged each individual believer to work out his or her own salvation, not in isolation and self-sufficiency, but always in relation to
the insights and counsel of the other members of the community.
Each believer was called to serve as priest to everyone but himself
or herself. It was this circle of support and encouragement that
enabled each individual Christian to act both freely and responsibly.

   This doctrine has immense importance for every Protestant
discussion of both the meaning and limits of individual freedom—in such issues as terminal treatment—and the complexities
of building consensus and community among diverse, self-interested individuals without the benefit of any fixed, absolute authority. The work of the Protestant ethicists and theologians described in the following pages continues to be informed and
animated by Luther's original doctrine of the priesthood of every
believer. For each thinker, the question remains the same: In
making life-and-death treatment decisions, how can we be true to
ourselves and, at the same time, faithful to those around us?

Deciding to Forego Treatment

Twentieth-century Protestant responses to the ethical crises
caused by breakthroughs in life-sustaining treatment have ranged
from American fundamentalists uncritical affirmation of the
state's interest in always preserving life to ethicist Joseph Fletcher's
radical situationalism, which defines the highest good as "human
happiness and well-being," not the continuation of life. An extreme statement of the Protestant affirmation of individual autonomy, Fletcher's position "comes down to the belief that our moral
acts, including suicide and mercy killing, are right or wrong depending on the consequences aimed at . . . , and that the consequences are good or evil according to whether and how much
they serve human values."[4]

   At times, however, Fletcher's position—in regard to patients
faced with the most difficult and troubling choices of all (such as
suicide and active euthanasia)—seems less a situational ethic (in

the sense of defending the needs and rights of each unique patient in each unique situation) than a sustained, nonsituational apology for each patient's right to die.

More consistent attention to the real, lived experiences of dying patients can be found in the works of theologian Karl Barth and ethicist Paul Ramsey. With his unyielding respect for the sanctity of each human life, however horribly disfigured or racked by pain and disease, Barth strained stubbornly against the voluntary relinquishment of life in any situation. One should never "give up" on another human being, he reasoned, since each life is of inestimable value to the God who created us all. Nevertheless, Barth's respect for and attention to the experience of each individual forced him to acknowledge that the uncritical application of this principle in all situations, regardless of the patient's wishes and condition, sometimes resulted in acts of physical torture and professional indifference that were anything but respectful to the value and sanctity of life. In the end, Barth wondered "whether the fulfillment of medical duty does not threaten to become fanaticism, reason folly; and the required assisting of human life a forbidden torturing of it. A case is at least conceivable," he acknowledged, "in which a doctor might have to recoil from his prolongation of life no less than from its arbitrary shortening."[5]

Throughout his work on medical ethics, Paul Ramsey has sought to translate Barth's insights into the actual circumstances and relationships in which end-of-life decisions are made. Ramsey agrees with Barth that we "need most urgently to renew the search for a way to express both moral recoil from any arbitrary shortening of life, and moral recoil from arbitrary prolonging of dying."[6] For the individual patient and caregiver, this can only be achieved, insists Ramsey, through an active and ongoing "partnership" between the patient and the person who provides his or her care:

> For this to be at all a human enterprise—a covenantal relation between the man [*sic*] who performs these procedures and the man [*sic*] who is patient in them—the latter must make a reasonably free and an adequately informed consent. Ideally, he must be constantly engaged in doing so. This is basic to the cooperative enterprise in which he is one partner.[7]

The uniquely Protestant insight of Barth and Ramsey for end-of-life decision making rests in their stubborn affirmation of the sanctity of both life and the lived experience of each individual, as well as the actual situations in which decisions are made and the relationships through which care is provided. For each, the ongoing partnerships through which decisions are made—without the benefit of absolute authority or preexisting theory—open patients and physicians to the challenge of difficult, sometimes traumatic, decisions. This challenge, both insist, can only be faced through the continued mutual attention and respect of all those involved in the decision-making process.

The Protestant View of Death

Almost all Protestant theology portrays physical death as a positive moment in God's order of things. The nineteenth-century German philosopher and theologian Friedrich Schleiermacher even asserted that human beings were created to die—that death is a perfectly natural completion to life, having nothing to do with either evil or sin. "Neither the Old Testament story," writes Schleiermacher, "nor the relevant indications in the writings of the New Testament . . . compel us to hold that man was created immortal."[8] Few other Protestant thinkers have gone this far, and most have continued to trace the origin of human death to the Genesis account of the Fall. Nevertheless, most Protestant theologians speak of death as an anticipated joy, the moment when believers once and for all cast off the pains and sorrows of earthly life and inherit the eternal, perfect life that Christ has prepared for them. In Luther's preaching and writing, the fear of death is a sin, perhaps the root of all sin, since it reveals that one doubts God's ability and willingness to save. "For where there is lust, sadness of heart, fear of death," writes Luther, "there the Law and sin are still present; there Christ is not yet present."[9] "There is something far worse than the onslaught and actual moment of death," echoes Karl Barth in our own century, "and that is an existence in the fear of death."[10] Speaking of our age's search for immortality through advances in medical technology, Barth speaks of an "enslavement to death" that makes "man grasp at such elixirs in an attempt to save himself from death and create life." "But," insists Barth, "this is not merely forbidden him but actually denied him. He cannot actually do it, and it is his salvation that he cannot."[11]

In this context, the problem becomes not the fear of death but the rejection of life. If life is so full of suffering and disappointment, and death leads to eternal peace and happiness, wouldn't it be preferable and desirable to die as quickly as possible? For most Protestant theologians, the answer has been, Yes but no. Death, however its origin may be connected with sin and the Fall, has been transformed by Christ into something entirely positive. Having accepted Christ, the Christian need no longer fear the end of life, but should welcome it when it comes as the fulfillment of his or her salvation. One still remains firmly bound to this life, but not out of fear of death. The believer continues to embrace life because, according to Protestant theology, each person's life is a gift with which he or she has been entrusted by God. Each day that one lives fully is a form of worship and a witness to God's graciousness and faithfulness.

According to this concept, death should be neither feared nor sought. Such a view of death as neither enemy nor free choice conflicts with the two extremes of the current end-of-life decision-making debate—on one hand, the urgency to delay death at all costs and on the other, the conviction that our lives are completely our own, to continue or discontinue as we see fit. For Protestant theology, the extremes to which many have gone to preserve physical existence, regardless of the person's potential for recovery or quality of life, betray a profound lack of faith. On the other hand, the readiness with which others would relinquish life represents an equally profound ingratitude and a rejection of responsibility, both toward God and other people.

In contrast to the clarity and confidence of Protestant theology, the beliefs and experiences of individual Protestants are all too often characterized by great fear and denial of death. A number of factors have contributed to this, but the unquestionable culprit for most has been many Protestant traditions' dramatic references to death and the judgment that lies beyond it. In the calls to repentance of many Protestant sermons, such as Jonathan Edwards's eighteenth-century "Sinners in the Hands of an Angry God" and R. G. Lee's recent "(There's Gonna Be a) Payday Someday," images of death and judgment are terrifying and over-

powering. Most listeners, whose exposure to Protestant belief is
through hearing sermons and not reading theology, miss whatever grander, subtler theological visions may be implicit in the
minister's remarks and carry away with them a single message:
death is a dreadful enemy, to be avoided at all costs. Children, of
course, are particularly vulnerable, listening in fascination and
terror to the minister's description of this evil spectre that haunts
the margins of our lives.

For those willing to probe deeper into their tradition, however,
the powerful testimony of Luther remains:

> So the heart learns to scoff at death and sin and to say with the
> Apostle, "O death, where is thy victory? O death, where is thy
> sting? The sting of death is sin, and the power of sin is the law.
> But thanks be to God, who gives us the victory through our Lord
> Jesus Christ" [I Cor. 15:55–57]. Death is swallowed up not only
> in the victory of Christ but also by our victory, because through
> faith his victory has become ours and in that faith we also are
> conquerers.[12]

Protestants trying to plan for the end of life have no easy
answers, no absolute authority, and no specific formula for decision making. For those who would look further, there is, however, a rich tradition affirming both the value of individual autonomy and the importance of respect for and responsibility toward
others. To be faithful to this tradition, end-of-life decisions are
based not on the fear of death or an eagerness to die but on the
patients' (or family's) free and responsible balancing of their own
wishes against the insights and concerns of those providing care.

DEATH IN THE ROMAN CATHOLIC TRADITION

Central to Roman Catholic doctrine about human life is the belief
that it is a gift of God, but it is not an absolute value. While God
has dominion over it, each person is called to be a responsible
steward of his or her life. Included in this stewardship is the
responsibility to take appropriate measures to protect one's health
and secure medical care when that is required. Also included,
presumably as an extension of the responsibility to secure medical

care, is the obligation to choose the kind and level of medical care appropriate to one's needs.

When the kind and level of medical care are excessively burdensome compared to their direct benefit to the patient, there is no moral obligation to obtain the treatment in question. In other words, the obligation exists only when a medical intervention provides reasonably acceptable benefits without imposing burdens, including cost, disproportionate to those benefits. For this reason, Catholic thinking has long distinguished between what Pope Pius XII described as ordinary and extraordinary medical means of treatment. The difference between ordinary and extraordinary is defined in relation to the condition of the patient, the expected results from treatment, and the probable cost to the patient, his or her family, and the larger community if treatment is given. Another term for *cost* here would be *burden,* which could include emotional and physical burden as well as economic burden. Where the benefits outweigh the burdens of a particular medical treatment—are "proportionate"—given the patient's diagnosis and prognosis, that treatment is considered ordinary. As a result, there is an obligation for the patient to secure it and the caregiver to provide it. If the burdens are out of proportion to the benefits, any obligation to secure or provide medical treatment ceases to exist. There is then such a thing as due proportion in the use of medical treatments. "Today it is very important to protect, at the moment of death, both the dignity of the human person and the Christian concept of life against a technological attitude that threatens to become an abuse . . . . From this point of view, the use of therapeutic means can sometimes pose problems."[13]

It is against this background that any discussion of Catholic teaching and the use of advance directives—whether in written form through living wills or in person through the use of a proxy—must take place. This traditional teaching demonstrates clearly that, in principle, there is no theological or moral conflict for Catholics who choose to draw up advance medical directives. Indeed, it might well be argued that responsible stewardship for one's medical care, given modern medicine's capacity to maintain unconscious human life indefinitely, often in a seriously compromised condition, includes the formulation of advance medical directives. But even if that is putting the argument too strongly, it does seem to be compatible with Catholic doctrine to say that advance medical directives are morally prudent measures.

According to Dennis Brodeur, a Catholic moral theologian, the church has not officially adopted a position either for or against the use of advance directives. As early as 1957, however, Pope Pius XII declared that the rights and duties of the family depend in general upon the presumed will of the unconscious patient. In the same vein, he declared, "The rights and duties of the doctor are correlative to those of the patient. The doctor, in fact, has no separate or independent right when the patient is concerned. In general, he can take action only if the patient explicitly, directly or indirectly gives him permission."[14]

To support this, Brodeur points to a 1986 statement of the Committee for Pro-Life Activities of the National Conference of Catholic Bishops on the Uniform Rights of the Terminally Ill Act. The act, drawn up in August, 1985, by the National Conference of Commissioners on Uniform State Law, was an attempt to establish uniform guidelines for the use of advance directives. While the bishops in their statement sought to limit the application of the act to patients in the last stages of a terminal illness, they did not reject the idea of advance directives or argue against their usefulness.[15] Their obvious caution comes from a determination to protect the value of human life as "the basis of all good .... The necessary source and condition of every human activity and of all society."[16] Consequently, the bishops' concern over anything promoting euthanasia, or their presumption in favor of artificially supplied nutrition and hydration, should surprise no one.

At the same time many bishops acknowledge how complex the issue is. "I am convinced that, from a moral point of view, the essential bond between food, water and life argues convincingly for the presumption that nutrition and hydration should always be provided. But I am also convinced that we are not morally obliged to do everything that is technically possible. In other words, there are cases when we would not be obliged artificially to provide nutrition and hydration."[17]

If the current official position of the Roman Catholic church, whether it originates from the Vatican or a national bishops' conference, is neutral, a more supportive approach to advance directives can be derived from practices typical in many Catholic hospitals and nursing homes caring for the chronically and terminally ill. If all of us, in the exercise of a responsible stewardship, must make decisions about medical treatment at various points in our lives, and if advance directives help us make these decisions responsibly, then it seems reasonable to conclude that the use of advance directives is compatible with the underlying principle of responsible stewardship.

Traditionally, Roman Catholics have grounded an individual's life in a community, thereby emphasizing a mutual accountability between individual and community. Excessive individualism, on the one hand, and totalitarianism, on the other, have therefore never been welcomed by mainstream Catholicism. For this reason, the family and the communal quality of life it reflects are the backdrop against which individual decisions, including those about life and death, are made. As Brodeur puts it, individuals have to make decisions about medical treatment, and those decisions need to be made in a communal context. Both proxy decision makers and written advance directives can take into account those contexts. A communal setting, normally the family, may take on other configurations. In the case of elderly people who are the sole survivors of their family, an increasingly common phenomenon today, the communal setting could be constituted by their close friends. In such a situation, they would be the most suitable people to make treatment decisions, thereby avoiding formal legal procedures such as the courts, unless as the very last recourse.

When it comes to the use of advance directives, traditional Roman Catholic thinking provides far more latitude than any of the existing forty-seven natural death state statutes. Statute law characteristically limits the use of living wills, for example, to those who are terminally ill or unable to make their own decisions and whose death is judged to be imminent. While those limitations do not present any major difficulty for Roman Catholics, such restrictions actually fall short of what Roman Catholics think is morally permissible. There is nothing, for example, that would require them to accept highly technical or expensive life-extending treatments, if the cost of those treatments placed unacceptable financial burdens on the family or the community at large. If we reflect carefully on Roman Catholic teaching in this matter, we must conclude that it gives considerable latitude for either personal or proxy decisions about withholding or withdrawing medical treatment, even when the outcome of those decisions is death.

With its emphasis on responsibilities mutual to the individual and the social community, Roman Catholic thinking in the United States has shown a preference for the use of durable powers of attorney for health care decisions over the use of living wills. Some of the early hesitation over living wills seems to have come from a fear that where living wills become widely used, a person without one could be deprived of a full range of medical options. Since new federal legislation—the Patient Self-Determination Act—prohibits basing the availability of medical care on a patient having or not having an advance directive, this fear now seems unjustified. There is another, more technical reason that appears to have prompted hesitation over the use of living wills. Decisions to withhold or withdraw medical treatment—particularly where the outcome may be death—are moral decisions. It is, however, impossible to make moral judgments in the abstract. To be significant, they have to be made in concrete situations. While living wills reflect the actual values and preferences of individuals, those values are being projected onto anticipated hypothetical situations. Some Catholic thinkers believe that this hypothetical approach compromises the moral quality of medical decisions written into living wills. Even given this view, Roman Catholics may draw up living wills, in the knowledge that they are compatible with the teaching of the Church. Indeed, American Catholics may be encouraged by the recent decision of the bishops of Spain to launch a national campaign to increase the use of living wills as a means of promoting a good death. The living will would be directed to family and doctors, among others, as a formal expression of the will of the dying person not to be kept alive abusively or irrationally, but to be allowed to take on his own death in peace in a Christian and human fashion.[18]

The moral integrity of a decision to accept or reject medical treatment when life is at stake requires the reconciliation of any obligations people might have to continue to live with the results of their decisions about the use of medical treatment. These obligations include the values and the goals that make a person's life humanly purposeful.

Decisions about medical treatment presume the patients' informed consent. Even in the case of terminal or irreversible illness, this requires accurate diagnosis and prognosis, in addition to an understanding of alternative treatments, with their relative benefits and burdens to both the patients and their family members.

The only way to bring the two together—the patients' personal values and the physicians' complete clinical assessment—is communication between patients and the physicians. If patients are conscious and competent, then presumably they can understand their medical situation and speak for themselves. It is when patients are unconscious or incompetent, or both, that communication with the physician becomes a problem. With advance directives carefully written out in the form of a living will, and with a surrogate appointed to interpret and execute them as the patient would, were he or she able to do so, the moral integrity of the decision required by Catholic thinking can be upheld.

The notion of responsible stewardship of a person's body and mind is then quite compatible with advance directives. Some Catholic moralists, like Brodeur, would go much farther. "The traditional form of a living will that requires incompetence and terminal illness before it is used or applied poses absolutely no problem for Roman Catholics," says Brodeur. He adds that there is no moral obligation for an individual to accept medical treatment that will not have a "proportionate" benefit. "So to have a document filled out that declares: 'In the event that I am terminally ill and incompetent, and all treatment is hopeless, don't do the following,' is a very reasonable extension of the church's traditional teaching that useless medical treatment does not have to be accepted or continued," Brodeur concludes.

A potential conflict between Roman Catholic teaching and the use of advance directives is raised by the issue of withholding or withdrawing artificial nutrition and hydration. This has become a contentious issue, seriously dividing Catholic opinion between those who view nutrition and hydration as basic human care and those who see these as another form of treatment.

The difference is well illustrated in the position adopted in 1986 by the New Jersey Catholic Conference when it opposed the withdrawal of nutrition and hydration from a thirty-one-year-old patient diagnosed to be in a persistent vegetative state. In a friend-of-the-court brief submitted to the New Jersey Supreme Court, the conference argued that there is a moral obligation to provide artificial nutrition and hydration. Since food and fluids do not cure disease, they cannot be considered a medical treatment. Moreover, the withdrawal of food and fluids will always lead to death. As a result, to withdraw sustenance is equivalent to directly intending the death of the patient. Without food and fluids, the conference maintained, it is not the underlying disease that kills the patient but starvation and dehydration. In effect, the withdrawal of food and fluids is a form of euthanasia, which is morally impermissible.

In his analysis of this brief, ethicist Richard J. Devine presents another Catholic perspective. According to Devine, the brief assumes that food and drink are the same as artificial nutrition and hydration. They are not. "This distinction is essential because it immediately negates the claim of universal need," he contends.[19] His point is that not everyone needs "a gastrostomy or intravenous lines any more than they all require a respirator or renal dialysis, but all require food and drink and air to breathe."[20] Conceding that artificial nutrition and hydration are essential to sustain the life of anyone in a persistent vegetative state, Devine argues that the respirator is just as necessary for the heart patient with pulmonary insufficiency, and dialysis for the patient in the last phase of renal failure. "Therefore the ethical principles governing the withdrawing or withholding of these procedures should be the same," he concludes.[21]

On the basis of this conclusion, Catholics could reasonably reject another assertion of the New Jersey Catholic Conference, namely, that food and drink are provided with no intention of curing a disease. Devine, for example, maintains that artificial nutrition and hydration are part of what he describes as a total medical effort to restore someone to health or maintain that person at a certain level of human functioning. When that effort, in its totality, ceases to have any medical purpose, artificial sustenance as an integral part of that effort also ceases to have a purpose.[22] If that is the case, it would be unclear why dialysis for end-stage kidney failure or a respirator for heart failure might be withdrawn or withheld, but not artificial feeding.

These conflicting points of view make clear that within the Roman Catholic community there is at present no official con-

sensus on the issue of artificial nutrition and hydration. This is
most clear in a statement issued in 1989 by Bishop John Leibrecht
of Springfield–Cape Girardeau, Missouri. Commenting on Nancy
Cruzan's case and others that involve the withholding or withdrawal of nutrition and hydration, Bishop Leibrecht said that they
could be approached in two ways. "First, there are moral principles coalescing around respect for human life: God gives life and
determines when it is completed." This statement, admittedly
simplified, leads to what Leibrecht calls "a valid Catholic position
which opposes removal of Nancy Cruzan's gastrostomy tube." Of
the two approaches, this might be considered the morally more
cautious view. "Second, there are moral principles coalescing
around respect for the person: God gives us not only life but
personhood and calls us to so develop our personhood in this life,
according to our means, that we shall have its fullness in the life
to come." Anyone adopting this line of reasoning, according to
Leibrecht, could morally approve of the removal of Cruzan's feeding tube.[23]

The conclusion that Bishop Leibrecht draws from this is
significant for Roman Catholics as they consider the morality of
withholding or withdrawing artificial nutrition and hydration.
"Unless there is an official and binding decision from church
authorities, Catholics would be mistaken to hold that only one or
the other line of Catholic moral reasoning is correct."[24] Since
neither the Vatican nor the National Conference of Catholic Bishops has yet spoken on the matter definitively, Catholics can, at
least within the framework of these two approaches, "approve or
disapprove withholding or withdrawing nutrition and hydration
medically inserted into the body."

As this discussion proceeds within the Catholic community, it
will be guided by the principle of benefit to the person and by the
law of God. "The context for judgements about what treatment
should be provided or may be refused for a family member, friend,
or patient is respect for the law of God and loving care for the
person who is ill or dying."[25] In determining the benefit of a
particular medical procedure to patients, one of the basic criteria
should be whether it will contribute to their "human functioning
so that they may complete their life tasks and achieve their spiritual destiny."[26]

DEATH IN THE JEWISH TRADITION

Jewish religious approaches to the acceptability and use of advance directives are framed by two powerful forces in Jewish thinking, *halakhah* and *aggadah*. Halakhah is the objective law laid out in the Pentateuch (the Five Books of Moses) and in the rabbis' interpretations and expansions over the centuries. Aggadah is probably best understood as the wisdom that has emerged over time from the application of the law, the stories of the Bible, and the tradition to the human condition. Together, the two create a productive tension by means of which Jewish religious thought has been able to combine unmovable principles with principled adaptation to changing circumstances and needs. "Halakhah grounds decisions in a system of principles; aggadah breathes spirit and reality into these principles. Halakhah defines 'how'; aggadah defines 'how much.' Halakhah looks outward; aggadah looks inward. Halakhah looks at the parts of commandments; aggadah looks at the whole of life."[27]

Together, halakhah and aggadah constitute an all-encompassing framework. As a result, even at the most extreme poles of a moral argument between Orthodox and Reform Jews, the central influence of the two forces is visible. "Both remain integral components of the ethical decision-making process."[28]

Within the framework, there is the central idea that God, as the creator of human beings, owns them. Consequently, humans enjoy the use of their bodies as something on loan. As Elliot N. Dorff, the provost of the University of Judaism, Los Angeles, California, explains, "It's as if you are the renter of an apartment. You don't have full ownership of that apartment."[29] The analogy also suggests that just as a tenant is expected by the landlord to take reasonable care of his or her apartment, the individual person has to take reasonable care of his or her body as something held in trust from God. For this reason, rules on hygiene, diet, sleep, and exercise found in the legal codes of Judaism are expected to be honored in the same way as the laws requiring care of the poor, for example. These rules are not just good advice for living longer or feeling better. Far from being at the discretion of individuals to follow or ignore, they are to be understood as divine commandments.

Judaism then does not extend to individuals' dominion over their own bodies, but it does hold them strictly accountable for proper care of the body. It is possible then for a devout Jewish person to execute advance directives, such as a living will, without appearing to assume a control that challenges God's dominion? More specifically, do advance directives, by means of which someone can determine the course of life-sustaining medical treatment in terminal illnesses, for example, open the door to suicide or euthanasia? Or is it possible to execute a living will and still respect God's absolute dominion?

These are, undoubtedly, serious questions for Judaism. Despite the concern they raise, however, the consensus seems to be that there is no inevitable link between the use of advance medical directives and suicide, euthanasia, or even physician-assisted suicide. "I think you have to reject the whole domino theory," says Dorff.[30] "Certainly it is possible that X will lead to Y and Z, and you absolutely hate Z. But that should not necessarily mean that you refrain from doing X." The fundamental point is that central to being a moral person is learning how to make moral distinctions. In addition, if any kind of moral conversation within a religious community is to be possible, there has to be the assumption that people can understand moral distinctions. "It's demeaning to virtually everyone else if you say that other people don't have the moral sensitivity to understand that something may be permissible, whereas other things which may even look similar are not permissible."

It is quite possible that an approval of advance medical directives to remove life-sustaining treatment might be construed as an approval of suicide. That, in turn, might mislead people into thinking that to abet a suicide or to commit one is permissible. "Obviously, you worry about this to some extent, and the product of your worrying should be to build an educational program to teach people the differences. Then you trust them to have the same kind of moral instincts you have. If they don't—and some don't—then you have to create the laws that enforce those moral instincts." Judaism forbids suicide. At the same time, it uses moral distinctions that allow people to see that removing life-support systems from a terminally ill patient is not the equivalent of committing suicide.

Within the Jewish religious tradition the phrase "terminally ill," while subject to some interpretation, has a recognizable definition. It is derived chiefly from medical criteria. In possibly its most conservative interpretation, "terminally ill" refers to patients expected to die within seventy-two hours. These are categorized as *goses,* or the moribund. Increasingly, though, it is becoming acceptable to include among the moribund those who have been diagnosed with a terminal illness from which death will result relatively soon, usually within a year, but possibly over a longer period of time. In these situations, while the terminal illness is irreversible, the patient is considered alive. "Therefore, any withholding or withdrawing of treatment from such people always comes with not a small amount of ambivalence and guilt."[31]

In a second definition, "terminally ill" means that the patient has been diagnosed as incurably ill and thus is considered analogous, but not equivalent, to a dead person. This category is known as *terefah.* While this view in no way lessens the sanctity of such a life, nor allows these patients to commit suicide, it does diminish the moral inhibitions surrounding the removal of life-support systems from someone in this condition. According to Dorff, a fatal illness detracts from the legal status of a person categorized as terefah, at the same time providing some flexibility to caregivers for terminating or withdrawing treatment. In clear contrast, all the laws as they relate to a person categorized as goses assert that he or she is alive.

Despite the long-standing existence of these categories and the framework they have provided for clearer thinking, uncertainty about the status of a dying person has been and continues to be common within Judaism. "For me, though," says Dorff, "the very existence of this confusion in the Talmud concerning the status of the terefah is just right: we are confused as to how to think of an incurably ill person, especially in the last stages of life, now more than ever."[32] But in assessing the two categories, Jewish religious authorities like Dorff believe that the terefah category provides a more useful approach to the issues contributing to the contemporary confusion over allowing the life of the hopelessly ill to end. In their view, it corresponds more directly to prevailing conditions in which medical technology is able to go to remarkable lengths to sustain biological life even though brain activity and affective responses have virtually ceased. In the face of such human ambiguity, it is not surprising that a corresponding moral ambiguity exists. The understanding derived from the use of terefah seems well suited to address both more effectively.

The patient, just the same, is at the center of this ambiguity, and Jewish tradition allows the patient a considerable measure of autonomy to deal with it. Decisions about treatment will naturally depend to a considerable extent on medical criteria, including the diagnosis, prognosis, and available range of treatments and their respective outcomes. But while autonomy does not extend to an absolute right to refuse medical care, it does permit patients to refuse any treatment they consider unbearable.[33] It also extends to choosing a physician, when there is more than one to choose from. This would, it seems, provide for a collaborative relationship between physician and patient increasingly favored in secular America. It would also support an environment being shaped by the patients' rights movement and the moral and legal need for all those involved to be accountable for medical interventions that now have such far-reaching consequences.

For these reasons, it should surprise no one that the general attitude of Jewish religious thinkers toward advance medical directives is positive. Dorff comments that "for the vast majority of the Jewish community, the answer is that we should have them because that's a way you can communicate, not only to the physicians involved, but also to your family, what kind of medical care you want."

Advance medical directives—in particular, the appointment of a surrogate for health care decisions through durable power of attorney—serve a number of purposes that are consistent with Jewish religious tradition. There is, unfortunately, a reluctance within families to talk in advance about medical decisions to be made for a dying patient. As a result, when those decisions, especially ones about withholding or withdrawing life-sustaining treatment, are being made, a family can experience both distress and guilt. This is true even in situations where such decisions, given all the options, are the most reasonable. "But the family members don't have to feel guilty when they, in fact, tell the physician to remove life-support systems, if the patient has said in a durable power of attorney that he doesn't want extraordinary means, or doesn't want these things to be used beyond the time it benefits him."

   Advance directives mean that family members are not abandoned to their own devices when life-and-death decisions need to
be made. They also enable patients to be responsible stewards of
their bodies, even in situations where they themselves cannot
participate in the actual decision. Within the Jewish tradition,
there is a strict obligation to seek medical care when it is necessary. For this reason, for example, Jews are forbidden to reside in
a place where no professional medical assistance is available. The
obligation to secure medical care continues even when the person
is dying and the medical situation is, presumably, hopeless.
"But," Dorff points out, "the goal of medical care at that point
does not have to be to try to reverse what the physicians say is
irreversible." On the contrary, it is permissible to accept the existing limitations of medical care and make whatever decisions
have to be made with those limitations in mind. In the Jewish
tradition, responsible stewardship of the body does not require
anyone to go to extraordinary lengths to obtain medical care.
"You may do that if you wish. If you have been diagnosed with
a terminal illness and you want to try all kinds of experimental
therapies and surgeries, the Jewish tradition would permit you to
do that even if engaging in those therapies involves great risk."
There is, however, no obligation to pursue such an extreme
course, not even when there is a remote chance that it might be
successful. Other, intermediate measures are morally acceptable,
says Dorff. "You are permitted to engage in hospice care where
the goal of the treatment is to relieve pain so as to make the rest
of the life you have, whether days or weeks or months, as comfortable as possible, and to live with family members to the extent
you can, rather than in a hospital." Significantly, this position has
been adopted not only by members of the Conservative and Reform Jewish communities but by a substantial number of Orthodox Jews as well. Assuming that state law permits the use of
advance directives to withhold or withdraw life-sustaining treatments once terminal illness has been diagnosed, there is nothing
in Jewish law to prevent someone from opting for hospice care
under these circumstances.
   The situation is far from certain, however, when the patient is
diagnosed with Parkinson's disease or Alzheimer's. While both are
recognized to be terminal diseases ultimately, they raise the question of whether and how one must provide food and water. Jewish

law does not permit the withholding of food and water from a patient. In their attempt to honor Jewish tradition while addressing the serious ethical problems surrounding the nutrition and hydration of patients, Jewish authorities, Dorff points out, have begun to draw a critical distinction. "I differentiate between food and water and nutrition and hydration in that food and water, as defined in the Talmud, are something which you ingest through the mouth. Nutrition and hydration may be ingested initially though the mouth with a swallowing action, but eventually they are provided through a nasogastric tube, and ultimately they are administered gastrointestinally. That no longer is food in the Jewish tradition." For this reason, there is a growing willingness within the Reform and Conservative communities to look upon artificially provided nutrition and hydration as another form of medicine. There are some within the Orthodox community who remain strongly opposed to such a view. Nevertheless, the vast majority of the affiliated Jewish community believe that, like any other medicine, nutrition and hydration can be withheld or withdrawn once a person has reached an irreversibly terminal stage of illness.

It is clear that the use of advance medical directives poses no fundamental difficulty for Jewish religious traditions. Indeed, there is ample evidence to suggest that within mainstream Judaism, advance directives can be considered not only permissible but advisable within the broad concept of responsible stewardship. As Dorff points out, the Jewish tradition has had a long love affair with medicine. "It has not flinched from exploring and applying whatever could help people overcome illness, seeing this process not as an infringement upon God's prerogatives, but as aiding God in the process of creation."[34]

In the course of that long exploration and faithful application, the Jewish tradition has learned how to distinguish between sustaining life and merely prolonging the process of dying. As a matter of practical ethics, it has concluded that individuals are obliged to sustain their lives but are under no obligation to draw out their dying. In face of the power of scientific medicine, however, that distinction has become less certain. Advance medical directives, as the product of a sustained conversation between those who give medical care and those who receive it, are accepted by Jewish thinkers as a way of clarifying the question.

Jewish tradition also attempts to distinguish between therapies that are technically successful for a particular organ or system of the patient and those that are truly beneficial to the patient as a whole person as well. The centrality of the patient and his or her medical benefit as the overriding criterion for distinguishing between the two in the Jewish tradition makes this distinction important. All this thoughtful exploration enables Jews to honor a religious tradition of responsible stewardship of the body while they adapt to the unprecedented possibilities of scientific and technological medicine.

> What the Living Will makes possible is the giving of the privilege to the patient himself to stop those things 'that delay the soul's leaving the body.' The developments of medical technology have caused problems which our ancestors could hardly have foreseen. We must not forget, in our loyalty to tradition, the welfare of the suffering patient who, when the Giver of Life has proclaimed the end of his earthly existence, should be allowed to die in spite of our machines.[35]

DEATH IN THE BUDDHIST TRADITION

The Buddha is said to have told his followers not to commit suicide. However, if a monk is seriously ill and sees the other monks being burdened by their nursing care for him, he may feel compassion for them. He may then contemplate his life span and, finding that he is not going to live long, stop eating, clothing himself properly, and taking medicine. Suicide then may be excusable.

According to Philip Kapleau, the founder of the Zen Center in Rochester, New York, "The Zen masters saw life and death as an unbroken continuum, the swinging of an eternal pendulum."[36] Put another way, there is no difference between life and death for Buddhists, since both are illusions. The Reverend John Daido Loori, the abbot of the Zen Mountain Monastery in New York, points out that in Buddhism "we call life the unborn and death the unextinguished."[37] Loori adds that the basis for this statement is the belief that, in being born, not a particle is added, and in death not an atom is lost. "That is, Buddhists, when they realize themselves and what the teachings teach, understand that who they are is the totality of the phenomenal universe."

When Buddhists examine life and death, they do so in the absence of a belief in God. Unlike Judaism or Christianity, Buddhism is a religion in which the question of God's existence is irrelevant to leading an ethical life. Instead, ultimate authority and, as a result, final responsibility for conduct rest with the individual. No doubt that explains the absolute centrality of *karma,* or the law of cause and effect, a critical characteristic of which is its power to propagate itself in the manner of a chain reaction, in this and successive lives. "Whatever the action that one takes, whether moral or immoral, it will have its karmic consequences," says Loori.

The basis of the Buddhist moral order is very different from that of the Greco-Roman or Judeo-Christian moral order. Christmas Humphrey, the author of *Buddhism,* writes that "the Buddhist . . . replaces Nemesis and Providence, Kismet, Destiny and Fate, with a natural law, by his knowledge of which he moulds his future hour by hour."[38] While the Christian believes that what people have sown, they will in time reap (Job 4:8), the Buddhist declares that what people reap, they have already sown. For this reason, Humphreys concludes that an understanding of the law of karma leads to self-reliance: "For in proportion as we understand its operation we cease to complain of our circumstances, and cease from turning with the weakness of a child to a man-made God to save us from the natural consequences of our acts."[39] Buddhism is both nontheistic and nonfatalistic.

Against this background, it should not be difficult to see that for a Buddhist it would be most important to enter death, like any other human activity, with care and preparation. And for this reason Kathleen Nolan, M.D., a visiting associate for medicine at the Hastings Center in New York, believes that Buddhism would have much in its teachings to encourage the kind of autonomous behavior involved in executing an advance medical directive. "The individual's own choices about the use of medical technology would be very strongly supported, as would the delegation of that decision-making authority to a family member, if the patient were unable to make decisions personally."[40] Nolan adds that Buddhism would appreciate the legal support provided by advance directive and health care proxy laws for something that it has always taught, namely, that individuals should enter death in a way that prevents it from being something bad for them or their family members.

The notion of entering death, or embracing it, immediately raises the question of where to draw a line so that embracing death when it is inevitable does not become embracing death when it is avoidable, that is, allowing an underlying fatal disease to run its course as distinct from actively taking one's life. Regarding the first, there is nothing in Buddhist teachings that obliges individuals to subject themselves to any particular life-sustaining medical technology. "In so far as we are talking about limiting medical interventions rather than actively killing oneself, I do not think there would be a medical technology that a person would have to accept," says Nolan. Regarding the second, there is a precept against killing, and that precept is very central to Buddhism.

In drawing the differences between allowing oneself to die and actively seeking one's death, the Buddhist tradition would use the principle of compassion. In a situation where the use of medical technology served only to prolong the process of dying, such use would not be necessary, since prolonging death is not compassionate. By extension, the principle of compassion would also allow room for dying individuals to consider the effects of the situation on their family. In this way, according to Nolan, "the notion of balancing benefits and burdens (of continued medical treatment and the consequent prolongation of dying) would fit very nicely with the Buddhist notion of compassion."

Given the law of karma, the way in which the individual dies can have profound meaning for Buddhists. "Letting go and dying simply is an ideal within Buddhism." As a result, for Buddhists who are well prepared to enter into dying, there could be a conflict between the clinical need for pain management and sedation that can result, and the desire to die consciously. Not surprisingly then, many Buddhists would want to use drugs sparingly so that they could be aware of what is going on during their illness and at the time of death itself. Nolan suggests, for this reason, that individual Buddhists should be clear in their own minds and in statements to physicians about how importantly they view the Buddhist ideal of dying, so as to balance this with their capacity for pain and their need for pain therapy.

This is not to suggest that Buddhists have an obligation to endure pain, if that is itself distracting from being in harmony existentially during a serious illness or at the time of death. At the same time, there is an aspiration to control one's dying so that it is the individual who *actively lets go,* and not medication that serves to kill the patient. For the Buddhist, the goal is to live one's life at every moment of one's life, including the moment of one's death. A model of this, according to Nolan, is the long-standing tradition of the Zen master who anticipates that death is approaching, writes a death poem of farewell, and then breathes his last by simply letting go. "That is the ideal. One is in such harmony with oneself that dying is nothing out of the ordinary, in a sense. It's just one of the steps along the path in one's life."

Along with the ideal of dying by simply letting go, there is the injunction that one's dying not be wholly selfish or self-centered. This too seems to come from the law of karma. "Even as the causes generated by one man react upon that man, so the mass causation of a group, be it family, society or nation, reacts upon that group as such, and upon all whose karma placed them at the time therein."[41] In dying, Buddhists may not overlook their responsibilities to others. "If people were accepting death or not fighting an illness out of a desire to duck their responsibilities, that would be seen as ego-centered and therefore discouraged," says Nolan. On the other hand, if people saw that their illness was having a bad effect on their family and friends, and for this reason rejected life-sustaining medical treatment, that would be acceptable on the grounds of compassion. Buddhists are held accountable not only for the effects their living has on others, but also for the effects of their dying.

Context is clearly a critical factor for Buddhists as they consider moral decisions. As Nolan explains it, the idea of simply saying that one does not want to be put on a respirator, for example, makes little sense in certain of the many schools of Buddhism, because that respirator would need to be evaluated in relation to the particular circumstances of the illness and the patient's actual condition. Nolan points out that this would extend to resuscitation or any other kind of medical intervention. "Statements such as 'I never want X or Y' or 'I always want X or Y' don't fit very well with the worldviews of most Buddhists who recognize the need for interpreting the precepts in light of circumstances." Giv-

en this identifiable morality built around context-specific decisions
within Buddhism, Nolan believes that most Buddhists clearly
would prefer appointing a health-care proxy to make medical
decisions rather than making absolute statements of preference
about particular hypothetical medical treatments.

However, some Buddhists are inclined to take the precept
against killing more literally and they may therefore be less inclined to withdraw life-sustaining medical technologies. The tendency would be to fight against, not succumb to, an illness in the
effort to prolong life. "As a result, such individuals would need to
be a little bit more careful about how they draw up an advance
directive, because they might not want to violate the precept
against killing by failing to take advantage of medical technology
that might help them." Still, most Buddhists would agree that the
precept against killing, though still very important, is only fully
understood when viewed through the principle of compassion.
That would allow one to interpret the prolonging of dying as a
violation of the precept against killing.

Without more explanation, the Mahayan view might seem to be
merely a clever argument that dodges the core belief. But as Loori
points out, the precept against killing is not just simply a rule. "It's
to be understood in terms of a double perspective." From the first
perspective, the precept is understood to prohibit killing anything.
"And when it says, 'Do not kill anything,' it means, 'Do not kill
a cabbage, do not kill a cow,' for the cabbage is life and the cow
is life, and the precept does not discriminate between higher and
lower life forms." Despite that, as Loori acknowledges, no creature on earth takes a meal without it being at the expense of
another creature. "We kill life, all of us, in spite of the fact that the
precept is in harmony with things. That's our karma."

From the second perspective, the precept calls for compassion
and a reverence for life. "What the precept says here is, 'Whenever
necessary out of compassion or reverence for life, kill.' If you
don't, you violate the precept." To illustrate his point, Loori cites
the case of a woman in terrible pain from terminal cancer who
begged her husband to withdraw life-support systems. He resisted
her pleas for quite a length of time, until one night he finally did
what she was asking. He was arrested subsequently and charged
with murder. "From the Buddhist point of view, he upheld the

precept. From a legal point of view, he committed murder. And the consequence of that accusation of murder is the karma of that action." Loori points out that had the man ignored his wife's pleas because he did not have the heart, or the courage, to kill her, he would have violated the precept. "That action would have been self-centered, and the Buddhist precepts are based on the ideal of 'no self.' " They are also based on the ideal of harmlessness, so that Buddhists are to conduct their lives in a way that causes as little harm as possible. Correct behavior, then, in a given situation—the time, the place, the position, and the degree—is that which will do the least harm.

Many Western Buddhists, including American Buddhists, are first-generation Buddhists. Consequently, in Western societies there is no widespread familiarity with the nuances of Buddhist beliefs and practices. Few caregivers know how to help Buddhists go through the final stages of a fatal disease. What is it that doctors and nurses need to know to honor in good faith the advance directives of their Buddhist patients?

According to Nolan, the strong affirmation of patient autonomy and of the need for medical information adequate for the exercise of such autonomy is very compatible with Buddhism. "Buddhism is based on individuals making decisions that are context-specific. The need for information is very great so that individuals can do that." Nolan also believes that caregivers must appreciate the importance Buddhists attach to the kind of death they have, and its circumstances. Buddhists believe that dying can be done well. Not appreciating this can affect the tone caregivers bring to questions about what to do in a serious illness or at the time of death. Despite the fact that Buddhism does not consider death as something frightful or bad, it may become a negative experience if those providing care do not understand the Buddhist view. For example, a Buddhist patient may be less willing to accept the side effects of sedation that may come with pain control because of a desire to participate actively in his or her life while dying. Being sensitive to such issues is critical, says Nolan. "I think if health-care professionals were conscientiously to involve their patients—keep them informed and develop a regimen that's compatible with the individual's responses to their concrete situations—they would have done well by their Buddhist patients."

Presumably, the same degree of sensitivity is needed when caregivers are working with patients' advance directives or their health-care proxies.

The Buddhist justification for this kind of relationship between patient and caregiver is derived from the principle of compassion. The original term for the Buddhist is *karuna,* which means more than empathy and suggests an ideal. "Karuna is a true sense of no separation. There's no caregiver, no care receiver; it's one reality." Loori explains that in this sense care is provided in a way that is effortless, and like growing one's hair, it requires no reflection. "It happens; if someone falls, you pick them up. And you do it as if you were doing it for yourself, because in fact you are, from a Buddhist point of view."

Health-care professionals may be inclined to consider Buddhism as something outside the ethical traditions that have shaped our medical values and practice. But Buddhism would echo Socrates' criticism of Herodicus for "lingering out his death." "He had a mortal disease, and he spent all his life at its beck and call, with no hope of a cure, and no time for anything but doctoring himself . . . and his skill only enabled him to reach old age in a prolonged death struggle."[42] Buddhism is also in sympathy with Cicero, who declared regarding natural law: "True law is right reason in agreement with nature; it is of universal application, unchanging and everlasting."[43] Finally, Buddhism has great affinity with the belief of Marcus Aurelius that "everything harmonizes with me, which is harmonious to thee, O Universe. Nothing for me is too early nor too late, which is in due time for thee."[44] It would be hard to exaggerate the influence of these great thinkers on the ethical traditions of Western thought. Similarly, faced with the challenges of high-tech medicine, it would be foolish of us not to value the Buddhist insight that "compassion is no mere attribute. It is the Law of laws . . . the light of everlasting Right, and fitness of all things, the law of love eternal."[45]

RELIGION AND THE EXPERIENCE OF DEATH

The preceding discussion of advance directives in various religious traditions makes clear that religious beliefs shape the decisions people make about treatment at the end of life. Death is the ultimate human experience, and just as religious beliefs have informed our conduct of life, so too will they inform the manner in which we might die. Since one of the claims of religion is to reconcile the fundamental contradiction between life and death in human consciousness, it would be a serious mistake to overlook the profound influence religious beliefs might have on the intellectual and emotional values of a person as he approached his own death.

What that influence might be has been explored here from the vantage point of some but not all of the major religious traditions. It was not possible, for example, to include the tradition of Islam. Despite such obvious omissions, the religious traditions that are included are sufficiently representative to provide in some detail the main characteristics of this influence. And despite the fact that some religious traditions have developed a more comprehensive body of philosophical and theological reflection on medical decisions at the end of life, it is clear that, together, they hold far more in agreement than in disagreement. For example, central to Hinduism is the belief that life is sacred and that suicide violates that sacredness. At the same time, Hindus are not opposed to ending life in a way that conforms with the natural order of things. Their preference when faced with medical choices of treatment as death approaches is to maintain life as long as that does not violate the basic principles of Dharma, which reflect what Hindus understand to be the law of the cosmic process. On the other hand, because they consider dying as something essentially religious, Hindus understand it to be a normal course of events in life. For that reason they deal with death in very realistic ways. The dying person is not placed in isolation in some antiseptic room. On the contrary, since he is undergoing a central phase of the life process, everybody in his family is involved. The religious traditions, as well as the medical tradition that is influenced greatly by religious attitudes, dictate that whatever practical can be done ought to be done. If the circumstances suggest that there is hope in keeping someone alive, then that is the thing to do. However, if it is a hopeless situation, in which the continuation of life means only suffering, then both religious and medical practice would be to let the natural process of dying take its course.

Because of their belief in the connection between the body and the soul, Hindus accept the obligation to care for their bodies as a necessary condition of spiritual well-being. According to Kenneth G. Zysk, assistant professor of religious studies, New York University, the whole premise of the Hindu medical system—*ayurveda*—as part of the Hindu religious tradition is the constant promotion of the health of the body. One of the concerns here is to maintain a harmonious balance between the body and the world in which it exists. This would, for example, explain the importance Hindus give to vegetarianism. "The culinary tradition itself is based on the maintenance of the body and a fundamental balance between the body and the cosmos."[46]

The obligation to care for one's body is, for a Hindu, more an obligation to himself than to any god. Hinduism places great emphasis on doing the right thing for oneself. The gods, such as Vishnu and Krishna, are there to be prayed to for assistance. But, ultimately, the individual views this obligation as an obligation to himself. At the same time, Hindus place very considerable importance on family members and their involvement in making medical decisions at the end of life. Traditionally, the eldest son has played a very significant role, especially in the case of parents who are unable to make their own decisions. Because of the centrality of the family in the Hindu tradition, it is clear that any exclusion of it from the clinical setting as death approaches would only add stress to a situation already full of stress.

The sacredness of human life, caring for the body which is viewed as a temple of that life, the understanding that death, as an integral part of life, has a time and place in the natural order of things—these are central to Hinduism as they are for the traditions described earlier. Therefore, as they approach death, Hindus are aware of the difference between warranted and unwarranted medical efforts to prolong life, as well as the obligation to care appropriately for the dying. The same is also true for the other religious traditions.

This religious consensus is not accidental and helps to confirm the important role religious beliefs can have in making medical decisions at the end of life. Religion can describe and explain the human condition at its most fundamental level. It can also help us make sense of ourselves and the world around us in a complete and satisfying way. "It reconciles us, at a deep, existential level, to ourselves, to our world, to each other, and, most of all, to our limitations and relative importance."[47]

There are questions which all the legal documents, all the rational discussions in the world will not solve. To answer these we must each turn inward, we must search for those few things that will remain meaningful when we arrive, as T. S. Eliot wrote, "at the still point"—between life and death.

NOTES

1. Martin Luther, *Lectures on Galatians, Chapters 1–4,* in vol. 26 of *Luther's Works,* ed. Jaroslav Pelikan (St. Louis: Concordia, 1963), 350.
2. Roger Williams, "The Bloudy [*sic*] Tenet of Persecution," in vol. 1 of *The Puritans: A Sourcebook of Their Writings,* ed. Perry Miller and Thomas H. Johnson (New York: Harper Torchbooks, 1963), 220.
3. Luther, *Lectures on Galatians,* 349.
4. Robert M. Baird and Stuart E. Rosenbaum, eds., *Euthanasia: The Moral Issues* (Buffalo, N.Y.: Prometheus Books, 1989), chapter 10, 92–93.
5. Karl Barth, *The Doctrine of Creation,* vols. 3–4 of *Church Dogmatics,* trans. G. W. Bromiley and T. F. Torrance (Edinburgh: T. and T. Clark, 1961), 425.
6. Paul Ramsey, *The Patient as Person* (New Haven and London: Yale University Press, 1970), 156.
7. Ibid., 6.
8. Friedrich Schleiermacher, *The Christian Faith,* ed. and trans. H. R. Mac-Kintosh and J. S. Stewart (Philadelphia: Fortress Press, 1928), 244.
9. Luther, *Lectures on Galatians,* 350.
10. Barth, *The Doctrine of Creation,* 288.
11. Ibid., 283.
12. Martin Luther, "Freedom of a Christian," in *Martin Luther: Selections from His Writing,* ed. John Dillenberger (New York: Anchor Books/Doubleday, 1961), 66.
13. Vatican, *Declaration on Euthanasia, Congregation for the Doctrine of the Faith* (Rome, 1980).
14. Pope Pius XII, "The Prolongation of Life," 26 November 1957, in *The Pope Speaks,* vol. 4, (1958), 397.
15. Dennis Brodeur, interview with authors, January 1991. All subsequent quotations from Fr. Brodeur, unless otherwise identified, came from this interview.
16. Vatican, *Declaration on Euthanasia,* 3.
17. Cardinal Joseph Bernardin, "Euthanasia: Ethical and Legal Challenges," *Origins* 18 (1988), 52 ff.
18. *Journal of the Pontifical Council for Pastoral Assistance to Health Care Workers* 14:2 (Rome, 1990).

19. Richard J. Devine, "The Amicus Curiae Brief: Public Policy versus Personal Freedom," *America* (8 April 1989), 323.
20. Ibid.
21. Ibid.
22. Ibid.
23. John Leibrecht, *Origins* 19:32 (11 January 1990), 525–526.
24. Ibid.
25. The Bishops of Washington and Oregon, "Living and Dying Well," *Origins* 21:22 (7 November 1991), 349.
26. William Bullock, "Assessing Burdens and Benefits of Medical Care," *Origins* 21:34 (30 January 1992), 555.
27. Claire Feinson, "Terminal Care and Advance Directives: An Halachic Framework for Analysis," in *Judaic Sources of American Law* (1990), 10.
28. Ibid., 11.
29. Elliot N. Dorff, "A Jewish Approach to End-Stage Medical Care," *Conservative Judaism* 43 No. 3 (Spring 1991) 3–51.
30. Elliot N. Dorff, interview with authors, October 1991. All subsequent quotations from Rabbi Dorff, unless otherwise identified, come from this interview.
31. Dorff, "A Jewish Approach," 21.
32. Ibid., 20.
33. Ibid., 12.
34. Ibid., 1.
35. Seymour Siegel, "Jewish Law Permits Natural Death," *Sh'ma* 7 (15 April 1977), 96–97.
36. Philip Kapleau, *The Wheel of Life and Death* (New York: Anchor Books, 1989), 10.
37. John Daido Loori, interview with authors, October 1991. All subsequent quotations from Rev. Loori cited in this chapter come from this interview.
38. Christmas Humphreys, *Buddhism* (London: Penguin Books, 1990), 102.
39. Ibid., 100–102.
40. Kathleen Nolan, interview with authors, September 1991. All subsequent quotations from Dr. Nolan cited in this chapter come from this interview.
41. Ibid.
42. Plato, *The Republic,* trans. F. M. Cornford (Oxford, England: Oxford University Press, 1961), Part II, Book III, ch. 9, 93.
43. Cicero, *De Legibus*, trans. C. W. Keyes (Cambridge, Mass.: Loeb Classical Library, Harvard University Press, 1966) Book I, ch. 10, verse 29, 329; Book I, ch. 12, verse 33, 333.
44. Marcus Aurelius, *The Thoughts of the Emperor Marcus Aurelius,* trans. George Long (Boston: Little Brown, 1892), 97.
45. The Voice of the Silence, as cited by Christmas Humphreys, *Buddhism,* 19.
46. Kenneth G. Zysk, interview with authors, December 1991.
47. Michael J. Wreen, "Autonomy, Religious Values, and Refusal of Lifesaving Medical Treatment," *Journal of Medical Ethics* (1991) 17:124–130.

For Further Reading

Address, Richard F., Ed. *A Time to Prepare*. Philadelphia: Union of American Hebrew Congregations, n.d.

Annas, George J. *The Rights of Patients*. Carbondale and Edwardsville: Southern Ill. Univ. Press, 1989.

Becker, Ernest. *The Denial of Death*. New York: The Free Press, 1973.

Desai, Prakash. *Health and Medicine in the Hindu Tradition*. New York: Crossroad, 1989.

DiNapoli, Joan Bridgers, and Hewitt, Furman. *A Practical Guide for Life and Death Decisions*. Durham, N.C.: Consultation Research, Inc., 1989.

Droge, Arthur J., and Tabor, James D. *A Noble Death: Suicide and Martyrdom Among Christians and Jews in Antiquity*. San Francisco: HarperCollins, 1992.

Glover, Jonathan. *Causing Death and Saving Lives*. London: Pelican/Penguin, 1988.

Grollman, Earl. *When Your Loved One Is Dying*. Boston: Beacon Press, 1980.

Jakobovits, Immanuel. *Jewish Medical Ethics*. New York: Bloch Publishing Co., 1975.

Kapleau, Philip. *The Wheel of Life and Death: A Practical and Spiritual Guide*. New York: Doubleday, 1989.

Kevorkian, Jack. *Prescription: Medicide, The Goodness of Planned Death*. Amherst, N.Y.: Prometheus Books, 1991.

Kubler-Ross, Elizabeth. *On Children and Death*. New York: Macmillan, 1983.

Levine, Stephen. *Who Dies?* New York: Doubleday, 1982.

Little, Deborah Whiting. *Home Care for the Dying*. New York: Dial Press/Doubleday, 1985.

Lynn, Joanne, Ed. *By No Extraordinary Means*. Bloomington: Indiana Univ. Press, 1989.

Meyer, Charles. *A Practical Guide to Caring for the Dying and the Bereaved*. Mystic, Conn.: Twenty-Third Publications, 1988.

Morgan, Ernest. *Dealing Creatively with Death: A Manual of Death Education and Simple Burial*, 11th ed. Burnsville, N.C.: Celo Press, 1988.

Morris, David B. *The Culture of Pain*. Los Angeles: Univ. of Calif. Press, 1991.

Nelson, Thomas, and the American Association of Retired Persons. *It's Your Choice: The Practical Guide to Planning a Funeral*. Glenview, Ill.: Scott Foresman, 1983.

Neuberger, Julia. *Caring for Dying People of Different Faiths*. London: Austin Co., Publishers, 1990.

Rahman, Fazlur. *Health and Medicine in the Islamic Tradition*. New York: Crossroad, 1989.

Ramsey, Paul. *The Patient as Person*. New Haven and London: Yale Univ. Press, 1970.

Reisner, Avran. "A Halakhic Ethic of Care for the Terminally Ill," *Conservative Judaism*, 43, no. 3 (Spring 1991), 52–89.

Rollins, Betty. *Last Wish*. New York: Linden Press/Simon & Schuster, 1985.

Sankar, Andrea. *Dying at Home: A Family Guide for Caregiving*. Baltimore, Md.: The Johns Hopkins Univ. Press, 1991.

Young, Ernlé W. D. *Alpha & Omega: Ethics at the Frontier of Life and Death*. Reading, Mass.: Addison-Wesley, 1989.

Veatch, Robert M. *Death, Dying, and the Biological Revolution*. New Haven and London: Yale Univ. Press, 1989.

Zysk, Kenneth G. *Asceticism and Healing in Ancient India*. New York: Oxford Univ. Press, 1991.

Resources

Choice In Dying, Inc.—the national council for the right to die
(formerly Concern for Dying/Society for the Right to Die)
200 Varick Street
New York, NY 10014

Dying With Dignity
175 St. Clair Avenue W
Toronto, Ontario
Canada M4V 1P7

Hemlock Society
P.O. Box 11830
Eugene, OR 97440

Hastings Center
255 Elm Road
Briarcliff Manor, NY 10510

National Hospice Organization
1901 N. Moore Street
Suite 901
Arlington, VA 22209

Wisconsin Cancer Pain Initiative
3675 Medical Sciences Center
1300 University Avenue
Madison, WI 53706
(This center can provide information about such initiatives in many
other states.)

Appendix A:
Sample Living Will and
Durable Power of Attorney

TO MY FAMILY, MY PHYSICIAN, MY LAWYER
AND ALL OTHERS WHOM IT MAY CONCERN

Death is as much a reality as birth, growth, and aging—it is the one certainty of life. In anticipation of decisions that may have to be made about my own dying and as an expression of my right to refuse treatment, I,

_____,
(print name)

being of sound mind, make this statement of my wishes and instructions concerning treatment.

By means of this document, which I intend to be legally binding, I direct my physician and other care providers, my family, and any surrogate designated by me or appointed by a court, to carry out my wishes. If I become unable, by reason of physical or mental incapacity, to make decisions about my medical care, let this document provide the guidance and authority needed to make any and all such decisions.

If I am permanently unconscious or there is no reasonable expectation of my recovery from a seriously incapacitating or lethal illness or condition, I do not wish to be kept alive by artificial means. I request that I be given all care necessary to keep me comfortable and free of pain, even if pain-relieving medications may hasten my death, and I direct that no life-sustaining treatment be provided except as I or my surrogate specifically authorize.

This request may appear to place a heavy responsibility upon you, but by making this decision according to my strong convictions, I intend to ease that burden. I am acting after careful consideration and with understanding of the consequences of your carrying out my wishes. *List optional specific provisions in the space below. (See other side.)*

Durable Power of Attorney for Health Care Decisions

(Cross out if you do not wish to use this section)

To effect my wishes, I designate _____,

residing at _____

(phone #) _____, (or if he or she shall for any reason fail

to act, _____,

residing at _____

(phone #) _____) as my health care surrogate—that is, my attorney-in-fact regarding any and all health care decisions to be made for me, including the decision to refuse life-sustaining treatment—if I am unable to make such decisions myself. This power shall remain effective during and not be affected by my subsequent illness, disability or incapacity. My surrogate shall have authority to interpret my living will, and shall make decisions about my health care as specified in my instructions or, when my wishes are not clear, as the surrogate believes to be in my best interests. I release and agree to hold harmless my health care surrogate from any and all claims whatsoever arising from decisions made in good faith in the exercise of this power.

I sign this document knowingly, voluntarily, and after careful deliberation, this _____ day of _____, 19 ____.

_____
(signature)

Address _____

I do hereby certify that the within document was executed and acknowledged before me by the principal this _____ day of _____, 19 ____.

_____
Notary Public

Witness _____

Printed Name _____

Address _____

Witness _____

Printed Name _____

Address _____

Copies of this document have been given to:_____

This living will expresses my personal treatment preferences. The fact that I may have also executed a declaration in the form recommended by state law should not be construed to limit or contradict this living will, which is an expression of my common-law and constitutional rights.

(Optional) My living will is registered with Choice In Dying
(Registry No. _____)

Distributed by Choice In Dying, Inc., 200 Varick Street,
New York, NY 10014 (212) 366-5540

HOW TO USE YOUR LIVING WILL

The living will should clearly state your preferences about life-sustaining treatment. You may wish to add specific statements to the living will in the space provided for that purpose. Such statements might concern:

- Cardiopulmonary resuscitation
- Artificial or invasive measures for providing nutrition and hydration
- Kidney dialysis
- Mechanical or artificial respiration
- Blood transfusion
- Surgery (such as amputation)
- Antibiotics

You may also wish to indicate any preferences you may have about such matters as dying at home.

The Durable Power of Attorney for Health Care

This optional feature permits you to name a surrogate decision maker (also known as proxy, health agent or attorney-in-fact), someone to make health care decisions on your behalf if you lose that ability. As this person should act according to your preferences and in your best interests, you should select this person with care and make certain that he or she knows what your wishes are and about your living will.

You should not name someone who is a witness to your living will. You may want to name an alternate agent in case the first person you select is unable or unwilling to serve. If you do name a surrogate decision maker, the form must be notarized. (It is a good idea to notarize the document in any case.)

IMPORTANT POINTS TO REMEMBER

- Sign and date your living will.
- Your two witnesses should not be blood relatives, your spouse, potential beneficiaries of your estate or your health care proxy.
- Discuss your living will with your doctors; and give them copies of your living will for inclusion in your medical file, so they will know whom to contact in the event something happens to you.
- Make photocopies of your living will, and give them to anyone who may be making decisions for you if you are unable to make them yourself.
- Place the original in a safe, accessible place, so that it can be located if needed—not in a safe deposit box.
- Look over your living will periodically (at least every five years), initial and redate it so that it will be clear that your wishes have not changed.

THE LIVING WILL REGISTRY

The Living Will Registry is a computerized file system where you may keep an up-to-date copy of your living will in our New York office.

What are the benefits of joining the Living Will Registry?

- Our staff will ensure that your form is filled out correctly, assign you a Registry number and maintain a copy of your living will.
- Our staff will be able to refer to *your* personal document, explain proce-

dures and options, and provide you with the latest case law or state legislation should you, your proxy or anyone else acting on your behalf need counseling or legal guidance in implementing your living will.

■ You will receive a permanent, credit card size plastic mini-will with your Registry number imprinted on it. The mini-will, which contains your address, our address and a short version of the living will, indicates that you have already filled out a full-size, witnessed living will document.

How do you join the Living Will Registry?

■ Review your living will, making sure it is up to date and contains any specific provisions that you want added.

■ Mail a photocopy of your original, signed and witnessed document along with a check for $40.00 to: Living Will Registry, Choice In Dying, Inc. 200 Varick Street, New York, New York 10014.

■ The one-time Registry enrollment fee will cover the costs of processing and maintaining your living will and of issuing your new plastic mini-will.

■ If you live in a state with living will legislation, send copies of any required state documents as well.

■ If you have any address changes or wish to add or delete special provisions that you have included in your living will, please write to the Registry so that we can keep your file up to date.

Appendix B:
State Law Governing
Living Wills/Declarations
and Appointment of a
Health Care Agent

Appropriate documents for each state are available from Choice In Dying, Inc.

Jurisdictions with legislation that authorizes both living wills/declarations and the appointment of a health care agent* (the District of Columbia and forty-three states: Arizona, Arkansas, California, Colorado, Connecticut, Delaware, Florida, Georgia, Hawaii, Idaho, Illinois, Indiana, Iowa, Kansas, Kentucky, Louisiana, Maine, Minnesota, Mississippi, Missouri, Montana, Nebraska, Nevada, New Hampshire, New Jersey, New Mexico, North Carolina, North Dakota, Ohio, Oregon, Pennsylvania, Rhode Island, South Carolina, South Dakota, Tennessee, Texas, Utah, Vermont, Virginia, Washington, West Virginia, Wisconsin, and Wyoming).

States with legislation that authorizes only living wills/declarations (four states: Alabama, Alaska, Maryland, and Oklahoma).

States with legislation that authorizes only the appointment of a health care agent (three states: Massachusetts, Michigan, and New York).

*The specifics of living will and health care agent legislation vary greatly from state to state. In addition, many states also have court-made law that affects residents' rights. For information about specific state laws, please contact Choice In Dying, Inc.

Prepared by Choice In Dying, Inc., 200 Varick Street, New York, NY 10014
(212)366-5540

About the Authors

Choice In Dying, Inc.—the national council for the right to die is now the largest and strongest right-to-die organization in the world, Choice In Dying has nearly 150,000 members in the United States. Another 300,000 contribute annually. Dedicated to ensuring individual freedom and compassionate care at the end of life, the organization works to educate physicians, nurses, lawyers, clergy, and the public.

Every year, Choice In Dying distributes hundreds of thousands of living wills and health-care-proxy appointment forms originally developed by the organization. Every day, its staff provides urgently needed assistance to families in distress and also advocates for patients' rights in the press, on radio and TV, and through its volunteers around the country. The organization assisted in the drafting and implementation of the Patient Self-Determination Act, which went into effect in 1991.

Choice In Dying was formed from the merger of two earlier organizations: the Society for the Right to Die, and Concern for Dying. For further information write to Choice In Dying, 200 Varick Street, New York, NY 10014.

T. Patrick Hill is the director of education at Choice In Dying. Born in Dublin and educated in Rome, England, and the United States, he received a B.A. and M.A. in history from Cambridge University and an M.A. in philosophy and education from the University of California in Los Angeles. Patrick Hill's articles have appeared in the *New York Times*, the *Christian Science Monitor*, *Commonweal*, and the *Hastings Report*.

David Shirley, formerly the associate director of education at Choice In Dying, is a freelance writer living in New York City. In addition to ongoing projects in the areas of AIDS and the ethics of patient care, he has written a biography of baseball legend LeRoy "Satchel" Paige (Chelsea House, 1992) and is currently working on a study of regional American music. He is also a regular contributor to *Option Magazine,* and lectures on "philosophy and clinical practice" at the Institutes of Religion and Health in New York.

Publications available from
CHOICE IN DYING, INC.
200 Varick Street
New York, NY 10014

For a complete list, with prices, please send a self-addressed, stamped envelope.

Set of Advance Directives (please indicate state)

Pamphlets

- About Medical Directives
- Medical Treatments and Your Living Will
- Nutrition and Hydration by Tube
- Making Life Support Decisions for Others: How to Determine a Loved One's Wishes

Books

- Advance Directive Protocols and the Patient Self-Determination Act
- The Complete Guide to Living Wills
- Options at the End of Life
- Refusal of Treatment Legislation: A State-by-State Compilation of Enacted Statutes (1991)
- Advance Directives and Community Education

Videos

- A Time to Choose
- In Sickness and In Health: Decision-Making in Long-Term Care (In three versions, for residents, for family, for staff)
- An Act of Self-Determination

Index